COLIN GARRATT'S
WORLD OF STEAM

COLIN GARRATT'S
WORLD OF STEAM

CONTENTS

Half-title   A Prussian-designed G8² 2–8–0, working for the
Turkish State Railway, steams out of Ereğli on the Black Sea coast.
Title   One of the former Rhodesia Railways 14A Class 2–6–2 +
2–6–2 Garratts romps northwards from Bulawayo.
This page   Some heavy hauling on Brazil's metre-gauge Teresa
Cristina Railway depicting a Baldwin-built 2–8–2.

First published 1981 by Octopus Books Limited
59 Grosvenor Street, London W1

© 1981 Octopus Books Limited

ISBN 0 7064 1506 X

Produced by Mandarin Publishers Limited
22a Westlands Road, Quarry Bay, Hong Kong

Printed in Hong Kong

All the photographs in this book were taken
with a Praktica camera using Agfa film

INTRODUCTION

To me, the steam locomotive—like the female form—is irresistibly photogenic.

Until the 1950s, the leading railway photographers depicted their subjects in a picturesque but predictable manner: sun behind the camera, a front three-quarter view showing the whole train in a pastoral setting and, ideally, a clean engine. Grime and industrial starkness were regarded as ugly. Black and white film was the only medium available for many years, and it is ironic that when railways were at their most colourful they had to be recorded in monochrome. Today the opposite is true; most photographers use colour but seldom in their history have steam trains been so drab.

The increased interest in railway photography over recent years has been accompanied by a broader and more enlightened approach; trains are shot from exciting new angles and are more honestly depicted by showing them as inherent elements of the industrial landscape. No longer is the photographer a slave to the sun; snow, mist and storm now add further vitality to his pictures. The demise of steam has added much to this way of seeing: broken-down sheds, grimy engines breathing their last gasp and graveyards make sad but poignantly dramatic themes. These new photographers see the steam engine as the most photogenic element within the remarkable industrial tapestry. It took a century for this to happen but for many years industrial subjects were not considered appropriate for artistic treatment, and the works of such painters of industrial scenes as L. S. Lowry were little cared for at the time.

The depiction of railways has been almost exclusively the photographer's preserve, few great painters ever turning to the subject. Over the last 20 years, however, more painters have taken up the railway theme, but, in general, their work is photographically orientated and unimaginative.

Although drawing freely from past traditions, I have tried to add an extra dimension of realism to my pictures and to show my subject as it is regarded today—as something outlandish and almost prehistoric. To eyes conditioned by the modernity of the late 20th century the steam locomotive is dated and utterly incongruous.

Perhaps the greatest single influence in my photography has been the golden summers of childhood spent next to steam main lines. This was my apprenticeship and those childhood visions are reflected in every picture I make. But, paradoxically, I turn to the painter for pictorial inspiration: to such unforgettable works as Turner's 'The Fighting Temeraire' and 'Rain, Steam and Speed'. Before my long expeditions overseas I go to the National Gallery in London to see these pictures and gain inspiration from their nobility of theme and grandeur of conception.

I hope that throughout the ensuing pages the reader will be able to share in my enthusiasm, and that the sheer magic of this lovely subject will shine through on the printed page.

STEAM
AROUND THE WORLD

For over a century railways were the major form of land transportation. Their unique role in fostering the industrial revolution and opening up the world's land masses is unforgettable. The steam locomotive was, of course, fundamental in this endeavour, and its almost supreme reign on the world's railways for 1½ centuries has left a legacy of interest and diversity that historians have yet to put into proper perspective.

Naturalists marvel at the diversity of wildlife (for example, there are some 8,500 species of birds alone), but a far greater number of locomotive types has existed. It is difficult to catalogue locomotives because, in common with many of man's creations, they are in a perpetual state of change. New designs, modifications and extinctions rapidly follow one another. In the natural sciences, however, the number of species remains reasonably stable, changes occurring in millennia rather than decades; thus, apart from a few extinctions, or the occasional new discovery, it is relatively easy to draw up a clear catalogue, which, when completed, remains more or less constant. Perhaps, one day, the necessary multi-volume work on the evolution of world steam will be undertaken, but in the meantime this book is intended to provide abundant and colourful evidence of the diversity of engines which can still be enjoyed.

Throughout its evolution, the steam locomotive changed little in basic principle. In outward appearance, however, the metamorphosis was considerable, ranging from the primitive creations of Trevithick—designed to take the place of horses on colliery wagonways at the dawn of the 19th century—to the ultimate in design and capacity, the 500 ton American Mallets.

A surprisingly wide spectrum of this evolutionary span can still be seen. The oldest engines left in commercial service are a pair of 0–4–0 tender engines built by Sharp Stewart of Manchester in 1873; while engines of similar vintage are few and far between, those dating from the 1890s and the early years of the present century are frequently encountered—both on main lines and in industrial use. Predominant among these engines are the products of late Victorian and Edwardian Britain, along with those of the 'big three' builders of the USA. At a guess, almost half of the world's surviving steam engines predate 1930, which in an age of inbuilt obsolescence and rapid technological change is a tribute to the pride of workmanship and inherent longevity associated with this subject. The largest engines still at work are the Kenyan 59 class 4–8–2 + 2–8–4 Garratts. These giants, which weigh over 250 tons in full working order and have a boiler diameter of 7 ft 6 in, are appropriately named after the highest mountains of East Africa.

The exact number of engines built can never be accurately assessed but probably exceeds three-quarters of a million. If we take this as an estimate and assume the average number of each type built to be 20, the number of different types approaches 40,000. A very rough guess suggests that perhaps some 40,000 engines remain at work today, embracing upwards of 2,000 types.

Although the steam scene has been documented in many areas of the world by parties of globe-trotting enthusiasts, and new discoveries are being made all the time, even in today's jet age the world remains a vast place: the railway, by its very nature, penetrated virtually every region on earth. Furthermore, the holiday-making enthusiast, keen to obtain value for money, tends to visit the countries where steam can be found in abundance and is thus well documented—such as East Germany or South Africa—and invariably ignores places where locomotives either are thin on the ground or are not definitely known to exist. Searching remote parts of the globe for engines is a time-consuming and costly operation.

Accurate documentation is further thwarted by the complexity of many railway systems and allied industrial networks. This, combined with language problems, makes it difficult to distil reliable information from railway administrations—especially where no inherent understanding of such research exists. Many railway managements regard steam as obsolete and irrelevant. When visiting various countries I often meet the motive power chief from the railway's head office in an attempt to assess the steam position, only to discover that I know more about the classification and whereabouts of their locomotives than the administrators do.

At a time when world travel is becoming ever more feasible, it is unfortunate that large areas remain inaccessible to visiting enthusiasts. This applies particularly to the communist states, which, ironically, are some of the biggest steam users. Today, almost all the countries of Eastern Europe, along with Russia, China, Cuba, Angola and Mocambique, place restrictions on serious study or photography. And few enthusiasts would be intrepid enough to visit such countries as Iran or Iraq—even

1

assuming that visas were available. In addition to the engines working in their totalitarian lands, Russia, China and some countries of Eastern Europe have emergent designs of their own, which, though descended from the main schools of practice, add a new dimension to our understanding of world steam practice in general.

Fortunately, the majority of countries welcome the visiting enthusiast, and, provided that the necessary authority is obtained from the railway administration, few problems, if any, are likely to be encountered. Indeed, many railwaymen feel a sense of pride that a visitor has travelled from afar to see his locomotives.

Although much remains to be seen, time is short and another decade will witness the disappearance of many older and historically significant types. Let us, therefore, review the current steam position by means of a brief synopsis on each of the five continents in their order of importance.

1   Typically British inside-cylinder 0–6–0 goods engines still work in Pakistan. Here one of these classic machines—superficially resembling the old Great Central J11 'Pom Pom' Class—receives the right away from Paktowal at the head of a freight travelling across the Punjab from Malakwal to Shorkot Road. The camel will wait patiently until the 0–6–0's 63-wagon train passes.

'sparks from a conventional engine
could wreak considerable havoc'

ASIA

Turkey, often described as the gateway to Asia, provides an appropriate introduction to the continent. Ever-increasing bands of enthusiasts are attracted to the country to savour the many British, French, German and American engines that work there.

The British *œuvre* includes ex-LMS Stanier 8F 2–8–0s left over from wartime service and some very racy looking 2–8–2s built by Robert Stephenson of Newcastle upon Tyne.

French locomotives are in dwindling evidence everywhere, but Turkey offers some delightful 2–8–0s built by Humboldt of Paris in 1912 as well as a class of 2–10–0s by Corpet Louvet.

Germany's contribution ranges from obscure 0–6–0 shunting tanks to such all-time classics as Prussian G8 0–8–0s and G10 0–10–0s; these are contrasted with typical German exports of the inter-war period in the form of huge 4–8–0s, 2–8–2s, 2–10–0s and 2–10–2s.

A hint of latter-day American superpower is provided by the Skyliner 2–10–0s from Vulcan of Pennsylvania, though rather more utilitarian are the ex-US Army S160 2–8–0s—the classic World War II design which was a descendant of the famous Pershing 2–8–0s of World War I. The S160s work in company with the German 'Kriegslok' 2–10–0s; thus British, German and American war engines all remain active.

Moving eastwards across Iran, with its locomotive graveyards, and through steamless Afghanistan, we reach the Indian subcontinent, which until 1947 was under British rule. Indian Railways is one of the best-utilized systems in the world and was closely modelled on British practice. With thousands of steam locomotives still at work, India provides the nearest approach to what Britain's railways were like during the steam age.

The country has three main categories of gauge: broad (5 ft 6 in), metre and narrow. Each offers a delightful pageant of motive power.

Highlights on the broad gauge include inside-cylinder 0–6–0 goods engines—the definitive British locomotive

2   Many of Calcutta's jute mills lie near the Hooghly River. The engine seen carying jute along the loading jetty to the waiting boat is a Fireless, which takes its steam from the factory boilers. Such locomotives are valuable for working in jute mills, where sparks from a conventional engine could wreak considerable havoc.

3

4

5

3 This metre-gauge veteran, named 'Mersey', has the distinction of being one of the two oldest steam locomotives left in commercial service anywhere in the world. She was built by Sharp Stewart of Great Bridgewater Street, Manchester, in 1873 and survives today at an Indian sugar factory. A sister engine of the same vintage works on a plantation nearby. When 'Mersey' was conveyed to Liverpool docks for export, Queen Victoria had another 28 years in which to rule her Empire.

4 A busy scene at a loading siding far out in the plantation which serves the Suraya sugar factory in northern India. After the cane from the plodding bullock carts has been loaded into the rail wagons, it will be conveyed to the factory by this lovely 2 ft 6 in gauge 0–6–2 tender engine built by Kitson of Leeds in 1900.

5 A shedman shovels up spilt pieces of coal into the characteristic wicker baskets at the Asansol steam sheds in Bengal. This depot is a last bastion of the mighty XE 2–8–2 and one is seen in the background in ex-works condition, having just returned after a major overhaul. These giants were the most powerful of the X Series standards and spent half a century hauling heavy coal trains over the hill regions of Bengal.

'mesmerized by a broad-gauge XC Pacific'

type. These are found right across the subcontinent from Pakistan to Bangladesh. Their close relation the inside-cylinder 4–4–0 also survives but is restricted to Pakistan; complete with 6 ft 2 in diameter driving wheels, this was the classic express passenger type of late Victorian and Edwardian Britain. Little less distinctive are the fabulous XC Pacifics ending their days working around Calcutta. These are the last big British Pacifics and they form part of the celebrated 'X' Series standards designed during the 1920s. In addition, a large stable of early 20th century 2–8–0s survive on secondary duties.

By far the most common engines on the broad gauge are the WP Pacifics and WG Mikados, introduced in 1947 and 1950, respectively. These classes represented a considerable departure from the earlier British traditions both mechanically and visually, as they incorporated American features. They were built in many countries, including India, and together total over 3,000 engines.

The metre-gauge sports similar American-influenced standard designs in the shape of YP Pacifics and YG Mikados, and sprightly speeds are combined with prodigious load hauling. These are supported by a diversity of older British classes of both tender and tank variety.

Some delightful narrow-gauge systems exist—a few privately owned. These offer all the charm and rusticity so beloved by enthusiasts. By far the most popular is the Darjeeling and Himalayan Railway, which climbs 7,407 feet to the former British summer resort with its commanding views of the snow-capped Himalayan ranges. The line, which abounds in spirals and zig-zags, was built by Victorian engineers; one of the original Sharp Stewart 0–4–0 STs remains in operation. In addition to Indian Railways stock, many other engines of diverse origins are found in industrial use.

Neighbouring Burma's metre-gauge network boasts a number of standard Indian types, including some outside-framed 0–6–0s based on the famous Assam and Bengal 'F' Class. An added bonus are the Garratts which work the hill lines to the north and east of Mandalay.

6 A cattle boy sitting on the banks of a Ganges tributary in Bengal becomes mesmerized by the passage of a broad-gauge XC Pacific decked in magnificent blue livery. This handsome thoroughbred, complete with 6 ft 2 in diameter driving wheels, was built by the Vulcan Foundry, Lancashire, in 1928; others came from the legendary shipbuilding firm of Beardmore on the Clyde during the early 1930s.

7

China remains an enigma to the railway historian; comprehensive information is not available and visits can only be made by package tour to certain preselected areas. However, it has been estimated that between 6,000 and 10,000 steam engines remain at work. China continues to be the only country still building steam locomotives, fears that this activity would cease after the devastation of the Tang Shan plant by earthquake during the late 1970s having proved groundless. In fact, 1980 was heralded by an announcement that a new design of locomotive classified 'Red Flag' and believed to be a 2–10–2 was due to enter service that year. What a marvellous way to begin a new decade!

Traditionally, China imported locomotives from America, Britain and Germany, but since the Communists assumed control Russian imports and home building have dominated. Standard classes consisting of Pacifics, Mikados and 2–10–2s have been built in enormous numbers over the last 20 years. One of the most famous is the QJ 2–10–2, based on Russian design. Several thousand are believed to be in traffic. The initials stand for 'Qian Jin' or 'March Forward'.

One can speculate upon what veterans might exist in the Chinese interior far away from the tourist belts. One dreams of ex-Great Western 'Dean Goods' 0–6–0s, Hungarian 4–8–0s and American 2–8–8–2 Mallets, to mention three random delights which could still exist, especially if one considers China's reluctance to dispense with anything that can be utilized! One visitor sighted a streamlined Japanese Pacific from the former South Manchuria Railway, and it has recently been confirmed that the British 4–8–4s exported by the Vulcan Foundry, Lancashire, in 1936 are also at work. However, even in this veritable paradise a sombre note was struck in 1979 when Chairman Hua announced a ten-year plan under which electric and diesel traction would replace steam.

7 The British built a brickworks at Ledo, close to the Burmese border, to service the collieries on the Assam coalfield. In this scene one of the 2 ft gauge Bagnall saddle tanks with 7 in diameter cylinder heads a trainload of freshly dug clay towards the factory.

8 Deep in the jungles of Assam, the British created a thriving coalfield after they had sailed along the mighty Brahmaputra River in Scottish-built paddle steamers. It was natural that Staffordshire-built saddle tanks should follow this enterprise. Here one is seen drawing a string of coal tubs from a hillside mine. The Lancashire boiler house, which provides power for drawing up the coals, is visible in the background.

9

9 Gangs of gaily dressed women hack clay from the earth near Ledo on the Assam coalfield. After carrying the clay in wicker baskets placed on their heads, the women load the wagons on the waiting train. The engine is a Bagnall saddle tank, originally built as an 0–4–2 but now running without its rear axle!

8

For sheer vintage steam the Indonesian islands of Java and Sumatra are without parallel. These islands were once part of the Dutch East Indies, though the engines reflect little of the former colonial power, the majority having been built in Germany. Exceptions are the lovely Pacifics built by Werkspoor of Amsterdam for Java and some very Dutch-looking 2–6–4 Ts of World War I vintage in North Sumatra. In all, the Indonesian State Railway has over 50 classes on its books, including steam trains and the last 2–4–0 tender engines, which, though a century old, still work passenger trains over a rickety weed-strewn branch line in Java. Twelve-coupleds vie with Mallets and compounds to form a variety which in terms of types per square mile has no equal. A modern foil is provided by the ultimate in Indonesian steam power, the 100 D52 Class 2–8–2s. These are latter-day imports in the German tradition, having come from Krupp in 1951.

In addition, a huge network of 60 cm and 70 cm gauge lines serve such industries as the palm oil estates of Sumatra and the sugar plantations of Java. Motive power is extremely varied, with 0–8–0 tender tanks, 0–6–0 Ts, 0–4–0 T and Fireless engines. Some 500 industrial engines are at work; most are of German or Dutch manufacture and date from the 1920s. Especially noteworthy, however, is the 75 cm gauge Hunslet 0–4–0 ST of 1971—almost certainly the last commercial steam locomotive to be built and exported by Britain. This humble engine ended a tradition almost one-and-a-half centuries old.

Of the remaining Asian countries, the Philippines merits the most attention, as the sugar plantations of Negros island offer a delightful assortment of colourful 3 ft 0 in gauge American engines, the legacy of that country's former political domination. Perhaps the most interesting examples on Negros are two 3 ft 6 in gauge vertical-cylinder Shays. One of these was originally built as a standard-gauge engine for the Missouri Lumber Co. The Shay, which is now almost extinct, was developed by Lima of Ohio and was the traditional lumber locomotive of the American Pacific north-west.

AUSTRALASIA

Australia's rich locomotive heritage—which until the 1920s was largely of British extraction—has passed tragically into history. Only three standard-gauge industrial systems survive; all use British engines and are located in New South Wales. One is for cement products and the other two are coal-carrying systems—the larger having a stable of 14 handsome Beyer Peacock 2–8–2 Ts. A few sugar plantation networks also remain steam-worked.

Little else survives; New Zealand is totally steamless, as is Fiji.

10 A scene on a Philippine sugar plantation with a cartload of freshly cut cane making a timely arrival at the railhead as a train of empty wagons arrives behind a 2–6–0 built by the American Locomotive Company in 1921. These carts, which convey the sugar from the private growers to the railhead, are hauled by water buffaloes known locally as *caribaos*. The green leaves on the top of the cart are the animal's food.

10

'waiting its turn of duty'

11 A handsome Pacific from the Japanese school of design seen waiting its turn of duty at Chia Yi depot on Taiwan's west coast mainline. Sent to the island during the Japanese occupation, this 3 ft 6 in gauge thoroughbred is of the Japanese National Railways Class C57 introduced in 1937. Taiwan retained several famous Japanese designs for some years after they had disappeared from their homeland.

AFRICA

South Africa, with its magnificent 3 ft 6 in gauge network combined with an idyllic climate and welcoming attitude by the authorities, provides everything the steam buff could wish for. Furthermore, the wild terrain and long-distance runs constitute what, for many, is steam's last fling in the great landscape of the world.

Prior to the 1920s, most of South Africa's locomotives were of typically British appearance, though more advanced in their wheel arrangements; the 4–6–0 became a standard type during the 1890s, and 4–6–2s, 4–8–0s and 4–8–2s were widespread by 1920. Many of these old lineages can still be found, either on secondary duties or following relegation into industrial service.

The shape of South Africa's motive power changed after the arrival of American imports in the form of huge 4–8–2s and Pacifics. These engines influenced the design of the standard 15F and 23 Class 4–8–2s, which together totalled over 350 engines.

The pure British element continued with the Garratt, however, South Africa being the principal user. A handful of beautifully proportioned examples survive from the 1920s, but today's visitor is more likely to see the GMA Class 4–8–2 + 2–8–4 of the 1950s—pugnacious beasts with a tractive effort of 68,800 lb. Imagine two of these double-heading a heavy train over a 1 in 37 bank in Natal, their eight cylinders issuing a mighty earth-shaking roar—the very stuff of steam railroading at its best.

South Africa's final steam design was a class of mighty 4–8–4 condensing engines for working across the arid Karroo desert. Capable of running for 700 miles without replenishment of water, these locomotives are 108 feet long on account of their huge tenders which contain the condensing elements. The system was developed by Henschel of Germany, who actually built the first engine,

12   The Karroo desert in South Africa is a vast arid expanse and a forbidding place to build a railway. For years problems were encountered with water supplies and special water trains had to be taken into the desert to replenish the locomotives passing through. The problem was solved with the introduction of mighty 4–8–4s with special condensing tenders which enabled the engines to run 700 miles without need for further water. Here one is seen amid typical desert terrain with a freight bound for De Aar.

'a forbidding place to build a railway'

13

13 South Africa uses Garratt locomotives for freight and passenger duties. In this scene from Natal one of the mighty GMA 4–8–2 + 2–8–4s heads away from Taylor with a morning train to Franklin. The GMAs are the largest Garratt class and 140 were built—in both Britain and Germany—during the 1950s. Despite their enormous power, these giants have an axle loading of less than 15 tons and are often referred to as branch line Garratts.

but the remaining 89 came from the North British works at Glasgow. The condensers are the only locomotives in the world with a pear-shaped front, and when running they emit a jet-like whine. Fifty noncondensing sisters were also built and these remain at work between Kimberley and De Aar.

The coalfields and goldfields support numerous interesting engines and among the purely industrial designs is a handsome 4–8–2 T of Scottish extraction. Many of these have been converted into tender engines and the hybrids resemble typical 'Colonial' 4–8–0s.

Steam still survives in Zimbabwe, a country which caught the western world's imagination during 1979 with the announcement that large numbers of Garratts were to be overhauled and returned to traffic. The Garratt has been prevalent in Zimbabwe for 50 years and today 90 per cent of the country's steam fleet is of this type. Just imagine the scene at Bulawayo sheds, where 50 huge Garratts might be stabled at any one time. The most elegant are the 15th Class 4–6–4 + 4–6–4s built between 1947 and 1952. Noted for fast running, these engines are frequently used on passenger trains. The largest are the 20th Class 4–8–2 + 2–8–4s, and with a tractive effort of some 70,000 lb and an operative weight of 225 tons they rate high in the power stakes of world steam.

Zambia has also been considering the restoration of some 20th Class Garratts after a period of almost complete diesel operation. Furthermore, a dozen South African 12R Class 4–8–2s were sent to the country during 1980.

The former Portuguese colonies of Mocambique and Angola are also steam users, but for reasons previously given, information is difficult to obtain. Mocambique uses both Garratts and conventional engines, but the fate of its celebrated Atlantics remains uncertain. Angola is world-famous for the Benguela Railway, which uses wood-burning Garratts decked in maroon on the hauls from Lobito on the Atlantic to the Congolese border 838 miles inland. The engines burn eucalyptus wood which grows in company plantations alongside the line.

The East African states of Kenya, Tanzania and Uganda have greatly reduced their steam operations over the last ten years but interesting survivors can still be found. Most engines are very British in appearance, as these territories were once part of the Empire. Engines are in maroon livery and many carry names: the Kenyan 59 Class commemorates East African mountains, while three classes of modern 2–8–2s and 2–8–4s—known collectively as Tribals—are named after local tribes. The design of these engines is based on the Nigerian Railway's River Class.

Kenya's 'Mountain Class' Garratts are the largest steam engines in the world, and for the last quarter-century they have worked the 330 mile drag from Mombasa on the Indian Ocean to the capital, Nairobi. During the course of this journey, the trains climb the equivalent of one mile in altitude. These engines are currently being displaced by dieselization but a few will survive as standbys.

In comparison with the countries already mentioned, the remainder of Africa has sparse steam workings. Zaire has a few active engines, while, on the west coast, Nigeria and Ghana both retain small fleets. Some of the largest countries—Algeria, Libya, Egypt and Ethiopia—are virtually steamless. The Sudan provides something of an exception with a fine stock of British power, the country's plan to annihilate steam traction by 1980 having failed to materialize. Pacifics, 2–8–2s and mighty 4–8–2s, all done in blue livery, can still be enjoyed and one can imagine how superb they look in a country whose background is predominantly yellow and gold in colour.

14

14 A baobab tree acts as a splendid frame for a Bulawayo-bound coal train storming away from Zimbabwe's Wankie coalfield, near the Zambian border. The engine is a 15th Class 4–6–2 + 2–6–4 Garratt built by Beyer Peacock of Manchester in 1949 to a design introduced in 1940.

15 Amid the wild Chaco scrublands of Paraguay grows the mighty quebracho tree, from which the world has traditionally obtained tannin for the processing of leather. Railways were built to convey the logs to the River Paraguay. In this scene on the Puerto Casado system the crew have arbitrarily stopped at kilometre post 27 to take their midday break. Their erstwhile steed, simmering patiently in the background, is a 2 ft 6 in gauge 2–8–2 well tank named 'Don Carlos', built by Manning Wardle of Leeds in 1916.

16

THE AMERICAS

Steam traction ceased long ago in North America but its memory lingers on in nearby Cuba, where as many as 600 engines—mostly of American origin—are believed to exist. Unfortunately, these engines are tantalizingly out of the reach of the steam-starved American rail fan.

In contrast, Latin America holds much to delight the enthusiast, albeit that most countries have a limited railway network and dieselization, combined with a general bias towards road transportation, inevitably means that the most interesting engines are thin on the ground and spread over a vast area. Scaled-down American power survives in Brazil, especially in the sugar-producing states of Campos and Pernambuco, where many former main-line engines are enjoying a further lease of active life hauling cane. At least two narrow-gauge systems in Brazil operate vintage American types, but the country's pride is the Dona Teresa Cristina Railway in the far south. This metre-gauge coal-carrying line is 100 per cent steam-operated, primarily by mighty Texas-type 2–10–4s which highball along at speeds of 40 miles an hour with 1,200 ton coal trains. The system conjures up visions of what the great American show would have been like in the heyday of steam. In 1980 the Teresa Cristina added to its roster by purchasing Santa Fé 2–10–2s from Argentina's Belgrano Railway.

Brazil's orientation towards American power gives way to a predominantly British aspect in Argentina, where most of the railways were built with British capital. The three principal gauges are 5 ft 6 in, standard (4 ft 8½ in) and metre. After nationalization, these were

16 A diminutive 600 mm gauge 0–4–0 well tank built by Orenstein and Koppel draws a string of empty wagons up to the mechanical digger at a stone quarry in central Uruguay. Notice the enormous crater the engine has helped to create during its eighty-year working life. This quarry is possibly the last in the world to be steam worked; the line is a third of a mile in length and the stone is used as track ballast on the standard-gauge Uruguayan State Railway.

grouped into five systems and named after generals. The 5 ft 6 in gauge 'Roca', which serves the fertile pampa to the south of Buenos Aires, was until recently working 2–6–4 Ts, 4–8–0s and Pacifics with three cylinders and a distinctly LNER flavour. Further south, 75 cm gauge Mikados from America and Germany trek out into the wilds of Patagonia on the 250-mile-long Esquel branch. Argentina also boasts the most southerly railway in the world, with the 75 cm coal line running from inland mines at Rio Turbio to Rio Gallegos on the Atlantic coast. The system is worked by Japanese 2–10–2s whose enormous trains weigh nearly 2,000 tons and are over half-a-mile in length.

Only a few classic British engines survive on the standard-gauge Urquiza, but the metre-gauge Belgrano sports a wide variety of power, with engines from Britain, Europe and America in evidence. During the early 1970s it was estimated that Argentina had 1,000 steam engines in service embracing 5 gauges and 80 classes. Although this situation has deteriorated greatly, there is still sufficient to merit a pilgrimage.

Across the River Plate in Uruguay the once-British system has fallen to a low ebb of activity. One shed I visited, however, had 20 engines present—principally

Edwardian 2–6–0s and 2–8–0s from Beyer Peacock of Manchester. Uruguay also possesses a stone quarry worked by a 60 cm gauge 0–4–0 well tank built by Orenstein and Koppel. This is possibly the last steam-worked quarry in the world.

The landlocked republic of Paraguay boasts two very different railway operations, both 100 per cent steam-operated. Pride of place goes to the standard-gauge main line, which runs for 240 miles from the capital, Asunción, to Encarnación, where, by means of a paddle steamer over the River Paraná, trains connect with Argentina's Urquiza Railway. This Paraguayan system is a genuine Edwardian legacy, complete with the original Moguls exported from Glasgow. The entire operation is wood-fired—even the lathes in the workshops which maintain the engines being driven by steam raised in the boilers of withdrawn locomotives. The other system lies hundreds of miles away, deep in the remoteness of the Chaco, where the mighty quebracho tree grows. This was the traditional source of tannin, and narrow-gauge lines were built to bring the logs to the mighty River Paraguay. The one surviving line is exotic; no trains need a whistle at night, as the engines throw clouds of crimson embers 100 feet into the air and the conflagrations can be seen from many miles away.

Sadly, the great transatlantic journeys behind steam are now a memory, but 20th century American power, built to the 5 ft 6 in gauge, remains active in southern Chile. The roster includes Baldwin 2–6–0s and 4–8–2s along with some 2–8–2s from Alco. Latin America's other landlocked country, Bolivia, is seldom visited by rail fans; with connections to Argentina, Chile and Brazil, however, the country has an interesting selection of motive power, including the last 4–8–4s on the continent and some French-built 2–8–4s.

Of the remaining countries, Peru offers the best variety, with some fine antiquities, especially in industrial service—but nothing as dramatic as the 1870-built Rogers 4–4–0 which, until recently, worked the sugar wharf at Puerto Eten.

17 A trainload of steel ingots trundles through a section of unspoilt country on its way from the foundry to the rolling mill at a steelworks near São Paulo in Brazil. The shunter sits unconcernedly on the rear wagon as the train rumbles over rickety weed-strewn tracks. The engine is a classic Scottish 0–4–0 saddle tank which hailed from Sharp Stewart's works in Springburn, Glasgow, in 1903.

EUROPE

Following the heartrending decline of steam in western Europe, the locomotive fraternity came face to face with the Iron Curtain, behind which steam thrives in abundance.

East Germany is alone among communist states in adopting a relaxed attitude towards enthusiasts, and the country has attracted many visitors to see such famous types as the Reichsbahn 01 Pacifics, the 44 Class three-cylinder 2–10–0s and the 50/52 Class 2–10–0s. Furthermore, the last three-cylinder Pacifics—the handsome 03^{10}s of 1937—can still be seen working expresses in the north. These delights are further enhanced by a liberal sprinkling of narrow-gauge lines.

Neighbouring Poland is by far the best European country for steam, but the variety has diminished over recent years and many older classes—notably the ex-Prussian P8 4–6–0s—are believed to be extinct. Some narrow-gauge forestry lines remain steam-worked—occasionally by the celebrated Feldbahn 0–8–0 Ts of World War I.

Czechoslovakia has recently retired its steam fleet, including the last operative Golsdorf designs. In adjacent Hungary some 19th century 0–6–0s with outside frames are active along with the lightweight 324 Class 2–6–2. Nowadays, however, most of Hungary's steam diagrams are dominated by the handsome 424 Class of mixed-traffic 4–8–0s introduced in 1924.

Steam working occurs on a lesser scale in Bulgaria and Romania, but Yugoslavia can still provide much activity. Although the Austrian classes have now disappeared from Slovenia, Hungarian 2–6–2s and 424 Class 4–8–0s contrast with the lovely Serbian 01 Prairies and German standard designs of the 1930s. War engines from America, Britain and Germany linger on in the form of ex-US Army 0–6–0 Ts, Vulcan 'Liberation' 2–8–0s and 'Kriegslok' 2–10–0s. Although not a signatory of the Warsaw Pact, Yugoslavia presents a daunting prospect to the railway enthusiast. The country's long tradition in welcoming holiday-makers is of no relevance, for once a visitor strays from the accepted tourist routes to look at railways, constant harassment is inevitable.

Little is known about the contemporary scene in Russia, but some steam has survived, albeit on secondary routes. In 1958 Russia was estimated to have at least 40,000 steam locomotives, many of standard designs built in vast numbers. The E Class 0–10–0s totalled over 10,000 engines, which makes it the most numerous steam class of all time. The SO and L Class 2–10–0s comprised 5,000 engines each, and the FD 2–10–2s and SU 2–6–2s totalled about 3,000 each. Additionally, many narrow-gauge forestry lines remain steam-worked—often with comparatively modern types. Regrettably, photography on any of the Soviet railways is virtually impossible.

'Victoria takes a breather'

18 One of the last havens of steam power in Britain was in dockland and Whitehaven became a noted location. Here 'Victoria', an 0–4–0 saddle tank built by Peckett of Bristol in 1942, takes a breather between spells of hauling coal wagons up to the boats from the surrounding collieries. In common with most Bristol-built industrial engines, 'Victoria' has outside cylinders and her short wheelbase enables her to negotiate the tight curves along the quaysides.

18

19

19 The last surviving Finnish State Railway 'Jumbo'—TV1 Class 2–8–0—shunts amid the snowy conifer-dominated landscape in the northeastern part of the country, close to the Russian border. The first of these heavy goods engines were built by Tampella in 1917, and by 1945, when the last were built, the class totalled 142 engines, some having come from Germany and Sweden. The type was introduced into Latvia when five were supplied by the Tampella works in exchange for linen.

20 The coal mining regions of northwestern Spain were a veritable paradise for vintage steam power. Here in the colliery yard at Ujo we see 'Eslava', an outside-cylinder 0–6–0 complete with four-wheeled tender, busily assembling rakes of wagons. This engine was built by Hartmann of Germany in 1882 for working passenger trains over the former Asturias, Galicia and Léon Railway. She passed to the Norte Railway in 1890 and was absorbed by the Spanish National Railways in 1941, prior to being sold for industrial use.

THE
BRITISH SCHOOL

When Britain pioneered railways, the industrial revolution was under way and the country was relatively developed in addition to being a world power. Railway building proceeded at a phenomenal pace, with reserves of coal, iron and limestone providing an abundance of raw materials. From 1830 onwards, British engineers spread the railway to all parts of the world and engines were either sold piecemeal or as a result of Britain building or financing the railway. During this period of railway expansion, Britain became known as 'the workshop of the world'.

The steam locomotive's character is largely dictated by its working environment. In Britain short journeys, serving densely populated areas, gave rise to a policy of light and frequent trains running over good track-beds. Accordingly, British locomotives were of moderate dimensions; and by the mid–late 19th century, the typical express passenger engine was either a single 2–4–0 or 4–4–0, and the ubiquitous inside-cylinder 0–6–0 had a virtual monopoly over the long slow-moving freight hauls that were so characteristic a part of the British scene.

Locomotive building in Britain was carried out initially by private firms; but as the main-line companies developed, they began to establish their own workshops, many of which became dominated by powerful chief mechanical engineers who bred a fierce individuality into the engines produced. These company workshops caused such places as Crewe, Doncaster, Swindon and Derby to become known as 'railway towns'. Although many thousands of engines were built in these works, they were solely for domestic use. The great export trade was conducted by private manufacturers, who were destined to make the cities of Manchester, Leeds, Newcastle and Glasgow famous throughout the world for the production of locomotives.

Many of the private builders built engines for the main-line companies (and also for British industry), but a high proportion of their output was exported. Naturally, the design offices of the main-line railways and those of private builders exerted a constant influence upon one another, and throughout the 19th century engines which were almost identical with those of the home railways were sent to all parts of the world—although many were scaled up or down to a different gauge. The doctrine was that what was good for Britain was good for the rest of the world too.

By 1900 the typical British locomotive had a copper firebox set between plate frames, a low running-board with deep splashers, inside cylinders and a boiler pressure of around 175 lb per square inch. Slide valves were universal, and it was not until the 1920s that outside valve gears became commonplace. The chief mechanical engineers of the various companies respected mechanical aesthetics with tremendous pride and no external excrescences were permitted to spoil the locomotives' shapely appearance, the mid-Victorian design concept of symmetrical outline being unquestioningly adhered to. The result was a beauty of outline never equalled. This contrasted sharply with many practices abroad, whereby locomotives were designed by a consortium of operating men and outside builders.

One has only to regard a Stirling 8-footer or a Robinson Atlantic to understand why British engines were admired almost as works of art. A few tried to emulate this perfection, and during the early years of the present century, Borsig of Berlin went through a 'British phase', as did builders in Holland and Belgium. In later years two American railroads became fleetingly mesmerized by the British aesthetic—notably the Baltimore and Ohio.

Britain's absolute lead in locomotive building ensured that replicas of the elegant designs were in evidence all over the world. By the turn of the century, however, competition began to loom large, particularly from America and, to a lesser extent, Germany. The huge transatlantic builders had a conveyor belt production capacity, and once their country's railway network was completed and demand from the home market began to level off, they began an aggressive export drive. By comparison, Britain's builders were small and manned by craftsmen who took an immense pride in their work and despised the mass production methods of the USA.

I quote a brief extract from a letter sent to *The Times* by the Glasgow locomotive builders:

'The American engine is designed with a view of reducing as much as possible the amount of labour in the course of its construction, and substituting machine work instead, and it is therefore a cheaper engine to build in works which are equipped for its construction than the British engine is in works constructed for the construction of the British engine. As to workmanship, we have reason to believe that the American engines supplied to this country were very far below the standard of workmanship obtained in the best locomotive works in Britain, and we have before us official information from India which goes far to show the same was the case in the Indian engines.'

The accuracy of these words remains evident today, and enginemen in many countries have told me how they prefer the old British classes for their inherent superiority. Nevertheless, the Americans did invade the traditional British market with rugged simple outside-cylinder machines with bar frames, steel fireboxes and an excellent steaming capacity. The price of these utilitarian locomotives was highly competitive, and whether they rode better, or would last as long, was not the ruling consideration; they were ideal for many situations. A result of this competition was the merging of three Glasgow builders in 1903 to form the North British Locomotive Company—the second-largest locomotive building complex in the world.

America's exports did highlight certain deficiencies in the traditional British approach, not least in the narrow fireboxes, which were often unsuitable for burning the poor-grade coal found in many lands. The American engines had excellent draughting, on account of their wider grates, which were built to dimensions unimpeded by coupled wheels and axles. Hot boxes and frame fractures occurred with certain British designs, and many felt that the bar frames and improved bearing surfaces of the American engines offered distinct advantages.

By the 1920s American thinking had exerted considerable influence, especially in Russia, Australia and South Africa, and although many of the last-mentioned country's engines continued to be built in Britain, they were to the transatlantic concept. Inevitably, Britain's export designs began to reflect these trends, and the famous 'X' Series of standard Pacifics and 2–8–2s built for India during the 1920s had wide fireboxes. By this time many of Britain's exports were bigger than engines used at home and wheel arrangements which were never seen on the domestic systems were being loaded onto the decks of cargo ships from many of the leading foundries.

In fact, by the 1920s Britain was nearing the peak of its domestic locomotive development. The 2–8–0 had been introduced in 1903 and was to become the general freight engine almost until the end of steam, as the 2–10–0 did not appear in widespread use until the 1950s. On passenger work 4–6–0s or Atlantics had partly superseded the inside-cylinder 4–4–0s of Victorian and Edwardian days; the graduation of the Atlantic into the Pacific produced the ultimate passenger type and, with relatively isolated exceptions, nothing larger was to appear. These developments were well behind those in other locomotive building countries. In America the Pacific was in widespread use during the first decade of the century, and by 1920 ten-coupled power was firmly established—as indeed it was in Europe.

Britain's final years of locomotive development were centred around mixed-traffic designs. The 1923 grouping had accentuated the need for standard designs amid the plethora of classes inherited from the private companies, while competition from road transportation meant that freight services had to be speeded up. The two-cylinder Moguls, formerly employed on mixed-traffic duties, gave way to a set of 4–6–0 designs with an average driving wheel diameter of 6 feet, such as the LMS Black 5, GWR Hall and LNER B1. A further advance on the Mogul was the LNER V2 three-cylinder 2–6–2; these were superb engines which combined a good turn of speed with an excellent haulage capacity.

One thoroughly British concept which must not be forgotten is the articulated Garratt—the most important variation ever made upon the traditional steam locomotive. The principle was conceived and patented by H. W. Garratt, who persuaded Beyer Peacock to construct his invention. When the first Garratt was built in 1909, articulated engines of several types were active—notably the French-inspired Mallet—and, although the Garratt was technically superior and did supersede its rival in certain areas, the two forms developed side by side until the end of the steam age. Traditionally, the Garratt was a simple and the Mallet a compound.

The Garratt's strength lay in the boiler being carried in its own separate frame and slung clear of all coupled wheels. Fuel and water were carried in separate engine units at either end on which the boiler pivots were mounted. Thus, the double-jointed engine provided absolute freedom for the design of boiler, firebox and ashpan, unimpeded by coupled wheels. The all-important question of weight distribution was solved naturally by spreading the wheels either side of the boiler.

Many railways around the world had—of necessity—been built with steep grades, sharp curves and light track.

In the early days, when traffic was of modest proportions, few problems were encountered, but as countries expanded industrially, heavier trains became necessary and difficulties were encountered in running larger rigid-frame engines. The Garratt solved these problems and was, in effect, a locomotive engineer's dream come true. It dispensed with the inefficiencies of double-heading smaller types; could be built to whatever proportions were needed; and was suitable for adoption on all gauges. Furthermore, its short fat boiler, with relatively short tube lengths, facilitated easy steaming.

As the Garratt colonized Africa, the Mallet became the ultimate power in America. There has been much conjecture on whether the Garratt principle—which was shunned by America—might have enabled more power to be gained from steam traction once the limit had been reached with the Mallet. The American Locomotive Company did show interest but, unfortunately, no tests were ever conducted.

Although principally regarded as a freight type, there is no reason why Garratts should not have been run at high speeds. Fifty miles an hour was a general maximum, although the French Nord did run one of the Algerian 4–6–2 + 2–6–4s up to 87 miles an hour on test.

The influx of American locomotives into Britain during World War II exerted considerable influence on subsequent home designs, in terms of both labour-saving devices and higher utilization between repairs. This also led to the elimination of splashers by increasing the height of footplating—a simple adjustment, but one which revolutionized the appearance of the British steam locomotive.

Following the nationalization of Britain's railways, in 1948, the twelve standard designs produced owed much to American thinking; all were simples with two outside cylinders. It was intended that the Pacific designs should have bar frames, but this proved impracticable at BR workshop level. All were designated as 'mixed traffics', except the heavy-freight 9F 2–10–0. However, these engines were capable of working expresses at high speeds and on many occasions their performances were little different from those of the Britannias. Although the BR standards retained some traditional symmetry of design, there was less to differentiate them from the latter-day products of America or Germany except, of course, size; the Union Pacific's 4–6–2 of 1903 approximated to the dimensions of Britannia although built half-a-century earlier!

And so the shape of Britain's exports changed markedly, the 'pretty things' giving way to more cosmopolitan designs based upon world experience, as epitomized by the Tribal 2–8–2s and 2–8–4s for East Africa; the Vulcan 'Liberation' 2–8–0s for Europe; and the mighty condensing 4–8–4s for South Africa. Even the Garratt eventually incorporated such foreign aspects as bar frames on cast steel beds and mechanical stokers.

The advent of larger administrations—in terms of both railway operators and railway builders—led to a freer interchange of information, and ever-increasing threats from road and air forced administrations into finding the common ideal. As far as Britain was concerned, efficiency was won at the cost of aesthetics and possibly workmanship also. Unhappily, the gains made were insufficient to save the steam locomotive in the land of its birth.

21 Very few Sentinels exist today. This example is at a wagon works in São Paulo State, Brazil. The Sentinel was a fascinating variation on the conventional steam locomotive and was the exclusive product of the Sentinel Waggon Works at Shrewsbury. This company had a long history in the production of steam road vehicles; in 1923 their attention was turned towards railway locomotives for shunting and short-journey hauling. Sentinels were fitted with a vertical boiler which was superheated and worked at a pressure of around 275 pounds per square inch. The cylinders were also positioned vertically and transmission to the wheels was by means of chains on a geared basis. The manufacturers claimed huge savings in running costs compared with the 'inefficiencies' of the conventional industrial engine, these savings being achieved by virtue of the Sentinel's superior boiler and transmission design. Some 850 were built—mostly four-wheelers—between 1923 and 1957 and they found favour in many parts of the world.

'these chunky 0-6-2 side tanks'

22

22   It was inevitable that several generations of British locomotives should have worked in Calcutta docks, but for some years now operations have been standardized around these chunky 0–6–2 side tanks which first came from Hunslet's Leeds works in 1945–6. In their desire to standardize, the Calcutta Port Trust resisted all temptation to diversify their locomotive fleet, remaining adamant that one type led to economy of operation by simplifying the spares needed. Furthermore, they required a choice of countries from which to order the spares. Accordingly, the second batch of engines came from the German builder Henschel of Kassel, with a final batch from Mitsubishi of Japan in 1954. The class totalled 45 engines, all of which were virtually identical in appearance. Here two of them are being prepared for duty at the huge engine sheds situated within the dock confines. Both are from the Japanese batch of 1954.

23 One of the most famous Indian locomotives was the XB Pacific, of which 99 were built between 1927 and 1931 for medium-range express passenger work. These engines formed part of the 'X Series' Standards, which consisted principally of Pacifics and 2–8–2s designed with wide fireboxes for coping with India's inferior coal. In general, the X Series earned a fine reputation but the XBs showed a tendency to distort the track and on occasions to derail. Although a 45 mile an hour speed limit was imposed, a serious accident occurred at Bihta in 1937, when an XB travelling over the speed limit left the rails. The severity of this accident precipitated the visit to India in 1938 of a special locomotive committee headed by William Stanier of the LMS and including such distinguished engineers as E. S. Cox. The XB's performance was carefully monitored and several design faults were discovered concerning the leading bogie, rear truck and drawgear between engine and tender. Modifications were carried out and the class continued to do much useful work, but they were seldom trusted at high speeds. The last survivor—No. 22153 from Rajamundry shed—is shown here on the day that she was withdrawn from service, having spent the last years hauling local trains around the coastal regions of Andhra Pradesh. This lovely engine was built by the Vulcan Foundry at Newton le Willows, Lancashire, in 1927.

23

24 Three o'clock in the morning at a remote plantation siding in Campos State, Brazil. The shapely 4–4–0 (see also Plate 32) is waiting for the wagons to be loaded with sugar cane. The pride taken in some of these vintage engines is a joy to behold, as witness the burnished brass fittings in the cab and immaculate exterior. Notice the muddy foreground strewn with sticks of sugar cane. These engines often have to run through a quagmire and not infrequently get bogged down—particularly high-stepping beauties such as this one with her large-diameter driving wheels.

25 An inside-cylinder 0–6–0 of the Pakistan Railways prepares to depart from Chalisa in the Punjab with a Dandot–Malakwal passenger train complete with a through coach for Lahore. The combination of engine, semaphore signals and station nameboard is guaranteed to make an English visitor feel at home.

26

26 One of the finest locations for industrial steam in India is the Suraya sugar factory in Uttar Pradesh. The fleet is decked in chocolate livery and two gauges are in operation; metre for connecting with the North Eastern main line and 2 ft 6 in for use throughout the plantations. The metre-gauge section is worked by the famous 'Tweed', an 0–4–0 tender engine built by Sharp Stewart of Manchester in 1873 and believed to be the oldest steam locomotive left in commercial service. Perhaps the most interesting engine in the 2 ft 6 in gauge fleet is this attractive 0–6–2 tender engine, built by Kitson of Leeds in 1900. She has a typical turn-of-the-century air and is a most charming engine to watch. She works in company with two British 4–4–0s, one from Dubs and the other from the Vulcan Foundry; both are of 1880s vintage.

27

27 Emitting a weird panting sound, the last surviving 0–6–0 + 0–6–0 T Kitson Meyer clanks towards the camera as it heads its final train. This dodo of Chile's Atacama Desert is seen symbolically against a sunset; the desert's golden hills have turned to black and the Pacific Ocean appears on the extreme right of the picture. This solitary engine outlived all its sisters and survived in this desert sanctuary until 1978, having spent 70 years hauling nitrates and gold from the interior of the desert to the little port of Taltal on Chile's Pacific coast.

28 The standard-gauge main line of Paraguay runs for 240 miles from the capital, Asunción, to the port of Encarnación, on the border with Argentina. Ever since its rebuilding to standard gauge during the early years of this century, the railway has used Moguls of typical Edwardian appearance, built by North British in 1910. More locomotives were needed during the 1950s and two further Moguls, based on the earlier design, were delivered from the Yorkshire Engine Company's Sheffield works in 1953. These engines are very LMS-like in their appearance. It is interesting that such conservative-looking engines should have been built at a time when the shape of British steam locomotives was changing so markedly. The two Yorkshire Moguls are named 'Asunción' and 'Encarnación'. Here 'Asunción' prepares to leave San Salvador with a passenger train to the Argentinian border. The emblem on the smokebox door refers to the year the railway was nationalized and British ownership ceased.

29

29 Most of Zimbabwe's steam fleet consists of the Garratt type, but these 12th Class 4–8–2s provide a notable exception. More than 50 were built, all by North British between 1926 and 1930. When Rhodesia—as the country was then called—was split up in 1967 and the northern part became Zambia, the 12s were divided between the two nations and some remain in Zambia today. These 4–8–2s were a natural development of Rhodesia's earlier 4–8–0s, as they allowed a wide firebox to be used on a powerful engine whose weight was spread over many axles. Stylistically, the 12s were descended from the earlier 11th Class introduced by the American Locomotive Company's works at Montreal in 1919. None of the 11th Class remain in service today.

30 Steam suburban trains are virtually extinct today, but in South Africa they ended memorably with some devastating performances by these North British-built 16 CR Pacifics of World War I vintage. Based at Sydenham depot in Port Elizabeth, these engines were used on the 21-mile runs to Uitenhage. Some trains consisted of 11 coaches weighing 350 tons gross, with timings of 47 minutes for the 21 miles, including 8 intermediate stops. It is said that unofficial speeds of 70 miles an hour were reached between stations only several miles apart. Pride of their crews, the locomotives were maintained in dazzling condition and included such embellishments as ornamental smoke deflectors, nameplates and various brass emblems. The 16 CRs are also used on freight duties. Here the flood waters of Port Elizabeth's tidal Swartkops River provide remarkable reflections.

30

31

31 In addition to Edwardian Moguls, Paraguay's steam railway can boast some period 2–6–2 tank engines built by Hawthorn Leslie in Newcastle-upon-Tyne between 1910 and 1913. The class totalled six engines built in unsuperheated form with slide valves. When these locomotives were introduced, the 2–6–2 T was little known in Britain. Today these 2–6–2s perform menial tasks and can be found working between Encarnación station and the docks, where the through coaches and wagons from Asunción are pushed onto the decks of a paddle steamer for conveyance over the River Paraná to the connection with Argentina's Urquiza Railway. Here is No. 5—one of the 1913 engines—at Encarnación with the name of her railway eloquently displayed on the tank sides: 'Ferrocarril Presidente Carlos Antonio Lopez', known locally as the Central del Paraguay.

32

32 I found this beautiful engine on a Brazilian sugar plantation. At first glance she looks American—an illusion created by the enormous balloon-stacked chimney. Closer examination, however, reveals her to be a British thoroughbred, complete with plate frames, low running plate with splashers and a glorious brass dome. Built at Sharp Stewart's Springburn Works, Glasgow, in 1892, this 4–4–0 originally hauled passenger trains over the metre-gauge Mogiana Railway before being sold into plantation service. How lovely she must have looked hauling trains of varnished teak coaches through the lush tropical scenery of Brazil's Atlantic seaboard. The engine is not entirely confined to the sugar fields, as she still undertakes long runs over the main line system to collect cane from far-flung plantations not connected to the factory by an internal railway network.

33 An 0–4–0 saddle tank drawing up to the Bessemer converter at the Indian Iron and Steel Corporation's Burnpur Works, which has just been charged with mixer metal. The engine was built on Tyneside in 1944 to a typical Hawthorn Leslie design which dates back to the early years of the century. The builder, however, was Robert Stephenson and Hawthorn, a company formed in 1937 by the amalgamation of Hawthorn Leslie of Newcastle and Robert Stephenson of Darlington. This new company continued to build to its constituents' design whenever required.

33

34

34 'David', from the Assam coalfield. This amazing little saddle tank was built to a standard Bagnall design and hailed from their Stafford works in 1924. 'David' has lost his cab and, indeed, his couplings too, and is having to pull his wagons along with an enormous chain. Notice the pressure gauge perched on top of the boiler. Over the years his boiler has become progressively weaker, and the steam pressure reduced accordingly. Today he only runs on 60 pounds per square inch and thus can pull just half the wagons he could in his prime. 'David' is one of a batch of 2 ft 0 in gauge Bagnalls supplied to the Assam Railways Trading Company over many years.

35 These glorious engines are the last big British Pacifics in the world. Classified XC, they were the heavy passenger engines under the Indian railways standardization programme of the 1920s. Introduced by the Vulcan Foundry in 1928, 72 examples were eventually built, the last 12 coming from the Clyde shipbuilding firm of Beardmore during the early 1930s. The XCs worked top trains over many parts of the Indian subcontinent before being displaced either by other forms of motive power or by the American-designed WP Pacifics. Today the remaining XCs are relegated to operating pick-up freights in the Calcutta area, although one occasionally heads a workman's train into Howrah. Never will I forget the morning I was travelling into Calcutta on a suburban electric. My train was running over a four-track section and we passed an XC working on the slow line. To see this handsome engine spinning its 6 ft 2 in diameter driving wheels was a thrilling sight and that magical instant recalled the past glory of the British Pacific tradition.

'the last big British Pacifics in the world'

36

36 When touring remote parts of the world in search of engines, unexpected discoveries can cause great excitement. So it was with this pretty Mogul, which I finally ran to earth, having chased it by jeep for miles through sugar plantation country in Brazil. She was one of 15 engines built by Beyer Peacock over the years 1899–1900 for Brazil's metre-gauge Leopoldina Railway. Little is known about these pretty engines, but the one shown here is almost certainly the last survivor. As a woodburner she was particularly inspiring to watch at night, for whenever she was under stress, clouds of crimson embers burst into the air while a ghostly wheeze emanated from the cylinder valves. Notice how the veteran's chimney top has corroded—the inevitable result of her constant fiery endeavours. The export of these locomotives coincided with the general advent of the Mogul in Britain, when 80 were specially imported from America because the home builders were fully occupied.

37 These magnificent 4–8–2 Ts are a familiar sight in South African collieries and are found in a splendid range of liveries. They were built by North British for industrial use and are a modern design based upon a long tradition of South African 4–8–2 tank engines. The Dickensian figure on the engine's buffer beam is the sand boy, who, for eight hours a shift, manually sprays sand onto the track ahead of the locomotive in order to prevent it from slipping when climbing steep gradients with heavy trains.

38 The Kitson Meyer was a strange double-jointed species and this one has a chimney at both ends. The front chimney emits dark oil smoke and the rear one pure white saturated steam. This last survivor of the type is working in the Atacama Desert of Chile. Built by Kitson of Leeds in 1907, these engines were fully articulated and were a close relation of the long-extinct Fairlie. The Kitson Meyer was superseded shortly after its inception by the superior Garratt and its advance was drastically curtailed. But for the advent of the Garratt, the Kitson Meyer would doubtless have become a prominent articulated type.

37

38

'the searing heat can be felt
a hundred yards away'

39 Industrial dramas of a bygone age, at Karabük Steel Works in Turkey, as molten waste from the foundry is tipped down what is known as a slag bank. Imagine the creaking of an upturned cauldron, the cataclysmic blaze of light, and the hideous crackle as the waste explodes. The searing heat is so intense that it can be felt a hundred yards away. It was the Turkish hero Kemal Ataturk who ordered this steel works to be built. Hawthorn Leslie of Newcastle-upon-Tyne received an order to supply saddle tank locomotives and six of these familiarly shaped engines form part of the company's motive power roster. They are built to a standard Hawthorn Leslie design, and are virtually identical with engines which once worked throughout Britain.

40

40 Nostalgia at the Howrah steam sheds in Calcutta as one of the Eastern Railway's XC Pacifics, done out in green livery, stands alongside a Class SGC 2 inside-cylinder 0–6–0. Both engines were built by the Vulcan Foundry for the East India Railway: the 0–6–0 in 1913 and the Pacific in 1928.

41 A rare ex-South African Railway's Class 8 4–8–0, now relegated to coalfield service in the Transvaal. The 8s were originally built for the Cape Government Railway as a mixed-traffic design. All were Glasgow-built—by either Neilsons or North British between 1902 and 1904. The 8s were the first major South African class to have bar frames and were descended from a batch of 2–8–0s acquired by the Cape Government Railway from Schenectady. They were subsequently built for other railways in South Africa and became important main line power for many years; the class totalled 175 engines.

42 The South African Class 6 was originally the 3 ft 6 in gauge main line passenger engine of the Cape Government Railway. They came from the Glasgow works of the three North British constituents (Dubs, Sharp Stewart and Neilson) between 1893 and 1902, and some 250 were built. Following the formation of the South African Railways in 1910, the 6 became a standardized main line engine until the never-ending quest for more speed and power caused the class to be relegated to secondary work. The modest proportions of the 6s rendered them suitable for such duty, and a few survived on the state system until the early 1970s. Others passed into industrial service like this one—a Dubs engine of 1897—seen delivering coal from Koornfontein Colliery to the nearby Komati Power Station in the Transvaal. The engine's incongruous colours are inexplicable, but the red running plate emphasizes the class's relatively large driving wheels of 4 ft 6 in diameter. Some members of the class had bar frames and these engines were characterized by a higher running plate.

41

42

'maintained in immaculate trim'

43 Chocolate-coloured engines are few and far between today, especially in the shape of such solidly built antiques as this Dubs 4–8–2 T, maintained in immaculate trim by the Witbank power station in the Transvaal. Originally this locomotive was a member of the Natal Government Railway's A Class, which comprised 100 engines delivered between 1888 and 1900. Dubs and Co. were founded in 1864 and became one of the great British locomotive builders of the 19th century, their famous diamond-shaped worksplate being a guarantee of excellent workmanship.

43

44 Throughout the 1970s, South Africa was a Mecca for steam enthusiasts, being noted for its busy main lines and wide variety of motive power. Today much of the variety has disappeared but survivors from many of the older classes can still be found in industrial service, and this fascinating 4–8–0 is a perfect example. Believed to be the only remaining engine from South African Railway's 13 Class, she was built by Neilson in 1902 and now works for Albion Collieries in the Transvaal. The engine's Edwardian contours are utterly captivating: she is beautifully rounded off, with not a bolt out of place, and epitomizes the indigenous British engines of the same period. The 13 Class originally consisted of 30 engines built as 4–10–2 Ts. They were later rebuilt as 4–8–0 tender engines but retained the side tanks, the six-wheeled tenders being taken from obsolete classes. Although some 13s passed into coalfield service in tender-tank form, all have now disappeared, leaving just this engine—which has undergone further rebuilding by having its side tanks removed and false splashers added. As with other South African rebuilds of tank engines into tender types, the splashers are filled with scrap iron in a concrete case, in order to provide the necessary wheel grip.

45

45   This magnificent locomotive is a superb example of a big
suburban tank, few of which exist today. Her proportions recall
the era of big tank locomotives in Britain during the early years of
the century. Although built in India, she bears the hallmarks of her
British ancestors. Classified WT, 30 of these 2–8–4 Ts were built
by the Chittaranjan works between 1959 and 1967, and the first
engine is named 'Chittaranjan'. Originally intended for heavy
suburban duties around Calcutta, the type has since become more
widespread. The engine illustrated is one of a stable based at
Rajamundry shed in Andhra Pradesh for working cross-country
passenger trains around the Godavari Delta.

44

47

48 The sheer power of the big South African Garratts is indicated by this picture of a 4–8–2 + 2–8–4 GMA Class preparing to leave New Hanover with a freight bound for Greytown. The GMAs, with their tractive effort of 68,800 pounds, provide the country's secondary lines with an extremely powerful locomotive, but to keep the axle weight below 15 tons, their water-carrying capacity has to be restricted to 1,600 gallons. Because of this, each engine is fitted with a separate auxiliary tank containing a further 6,750 gallons. It was common practice to double-head these GMAs over the steeply graded lines of Natal. Imagine a pair of them pugnaciously attacking a 1 in 30 gradient, the two locomotives separated by two water tanks and eight cylinders issuing a pounding roar. These activities constituted some of the most stirring steam performances of the 1970s.

47 The Zimbabwe Railway's steam fleet consists almost entirely of Garratt locomotives built in Manchester by Beyer Peacock. Operations are centred upon the huge Bulawayo sheds, where one may see up to 50 Garratts, embracing five different classes. Their heaviest duty is conveying coal from the Wankie collieries, near the Zambian border, and for this work the 15th 4–6–4 + 4–6–4 and 20th 4–8–2 + 4–8–2 types are used. Smaller Garratts in the form of the 14A Class 2–6–2 + 2–6–2s can be found on the lightly laid line between Bulawayo and West Nicholson. Here a Class 14A engine heads towards Bulawayo with a heavy freight. The train has just left the water stop at Balla Balla and the blowdown valve is fully open to eject sludge and impurities from inside the engine's boiler. The 14As—which are direct descendants of the 14th Class of 1928—were introduced in 1953 and total 18 engines.

46 A British inside-cylinder 0–6–0 labours through hill country between Malakwal and Dandot in the Pakistan Punjab. These engines are found right across the Indian subcontinent, from the Khyber Pass through to Bangladesh. The Pakistan engines are oil burners, as this dense column of black smoke clearly testifies: there are no coalfields in Pakistan.

48

49   It was rare for Andrew Barclay to build side tank engines for British industrial use, but this class, complete with 18 in cylinders, appeared intermittently over a 45 year period. This engine is one of the last survivors; she is fitted with a Giesl chimney and is seen assembling a rake of coal wagons in the yard at Bedlay Colliery, near Glasgow. The Giesl chimney was one of a number of sophistications introduced during the last few decades of steam, and although it was heartily adopted in certain areas by the National Coal Board, it saw little use on Britain's main lines. The brainchild of Dr Giesl of the Vienna Locomotive Works, the device was designed to increase the efficiency of the exhaust steam and thus lead to a reduction in fuel consumption and freer steaming. This chimney design was much disliked by railway enthusiasts on account of its unattractive shape. This is understandable, as a locomotive's appearance is greatly influenced by its chimney, and throughout locomotive history many engines have been marred aesthetically by successive chief mechanical engineers applying incongruous designs. The Giesl was regarded with particular disdain, especially in Britain, where the ruling trend has always been governed by some sensitivity towards outward appearance.

'a locomotive's appearance is
greatly influenced by its chimney'

52 This delightful 0–4–0 saddle tank with 14 in cylinders represents a much more typical Andrew Barclay design than that shown in Plate 49, the basic shape being familiar to industrial users throughout Britain and many parts of the world. She is one of the most modern engines described in this book, having been built at the company's Kilmarnock works as recently as 1954. Along with a sister, the engine actually helped to build this Bedfordshire power station, prior to starting its main function of delivering coal from the connecting sidings with British Rail. These oil-fired engines survived well into the 1970s. Their relative longevity was partly due to the fact that the power station superintendent's wife was a direct descendant of Richard Trevithick, who built the world's first steam locomotive in 1804; strong allegiance was felt when, nearly two centuries later, these Bedfordshire engines formed part of the rearguard of British steam.

50 An historic view of the last steam-worked ironstone mine in Britain. Located at Nassington on the Northamptonshire ironstone belt, it was worked by a brace of Hunslet's standard 16 in 0–6–0 saddle tanks, introduced in 1923 and forerunners of the famous Austerities. Nassington's engines were named 'Ring Haw' and 'Jack's Green', after two local coppices. 'Ring Haw' is here working in the gullet, in conjunction with the mechanical digger. Notice the depth of the overburden and also the seams of silica white sand which formed a by-product of the ironstone mining. Nassington represents the end of a glorious association of steam and iron in Northamptonshire—an industrial period which began in 1852, when Thomas Butlin smelted pig iron at Wellingborough.

50

51 A typical product of the industrial locomotive builders of Kilmarnock, from the town's most celebrated works— Andrew Barclay. The building of locomotives in Kilmarnock coincided with the development of the local reserves of coal and iron, and in 1859 Andrew Barclay built the first of a long line of saddle tanks. Over the following century they became famous for their four- and six-coupled designs. Other well-known Kilmarnock works were those of Dick Kerr and Grant Ritchie.

'a vibrant industrial tapestry'

53

53 A heavy-duty 0–6–0 tank engine built by Robert Stephenson and Hawthorn in 1948. The orange cloud drifting across the scene—a large steel works on the eastern coalfield in Bengal—indicates that a charge of ore has just gone into the furnaces, while the plumes of steam issuing into the air show that the coke quenching is active. This scene, set in a vibrant industrial tapestry, is a particularly fitting one, as the steam locomotive was born amid industry and in all probability it will die there too.

54

54 One of India's most distinctive locomotive types is the XD 2–8–2. Although now superseded by the ubiquitous WG, many Indian drivers maintain the superiority of the XD, in terms of both steaming capacity and haulage ability. The first ones came from the Vulcan Foundry in 1927, and building continued until 1948, with a break during the war years. The class finally totalled almost 200 engines and could be seen at work in many parts of the country. Although the XDs have neither the flamboyance of the Pacifics nor the power of their bigger brothers the XEs, they are a delightful engine to behold. Some depots on the South Central Railway continue to maintain them in superb trim. Until dieselization in 1968, XDs were operating 1,800 ton coal trains over the 77 miles from Dornakal Junction to Vijayawada in 2¼ hours—enduring proof that the steam locomotive is not the outmoded relic it is often stated to be! Today all surviving XDs are demoted to secondary duties. The engine illustrated, No. 22372, was one of the last to be built, having come from North British in 1946.

55 In common with Rhodesia, South African Railways made extensive use of the narrow firebox 4–8–0 prior to the introduction of the 4–8–2 in 1909. There were two principal phases of 4–8–2 in South Africa: the British design, with narrow fireboxes and plate frames, which reigned supreme until 1925; and the American style, with wide fireboxes and bar frames, which predominated from then until the end of steam. The engine seen here belongs to the British phase and is classified 12A—a type first introduced in 1919 for working 1,400 ton coal trains around Witbank. Sixty-seven were built for main line service, and so satisfactory were they that building continued in unsuperheated form for colliery service right up until the 1950s. With a cylinder diameter of 24 in, these large engines proved to be ideal for hauling heavy trains from the collieries up to the connection with the main line, as such duties in South Africa invariably involve several miles of running over steeply graded lines. This engine, working for New Douglas Colliery, is one of those delivered specifically for coalfield service: thus she provides a marked contrast with the usual practice of simply relegating obsolete main line types to industrial service.

55

57

56 The ex-LMS Black 5 4–6–0 epitomizes the British mixed-traffic engine. No fewer than 842 were produced between their introduction by William Stanier in 1934 and the building of the last examples under British Railways in 1951. They were capable of working express passenger trains as well as heavy goods, and many engine men maintained that they were the finest engines ever built. In fact, there was a very strong feeling during 1950—when British Railways' standard designs were being prepared—that the Black 5 should be perpetuated in unaltered form. In the event, the Standard 5 was produced, which in many ways was merely an updated version of this classic LMS design. The Black 5s could be seen all over the former LMS system and their distribution ranged from the Scottish Highlands down to the West Country. Only four were named. This is one of them, No. 45156, 'Ayrshire Yeomanry', seen amid the gloom of Patricroft shed in Manchester in 1967—a time when the nameplates of all surviving engines had been removed for security, on account of their high monetary value as collector's pieces. One of the related Stanier 8F 2–8–0s can be seen in the background.

57 Many of Argentina's railways were built by the British, the most famous being the Buenos Aires and Great Southern—affectionately known as the BAGS. This railway was instrumental in opening up vast areas of the fertile pampa to the south of Buenos Aires and in conveying millions of tons of beef and grain to the great Atlantic ports. The BAGS was worked by superb British engines, which survived long after nationalization in 1948, when the railway took the name General Roca as part of Argentina's policy to name them after generals. Three-cylinder engines—with more than a hint of LNER about them—were a speciality of the BAGS. Although, sadly, these have disappeared, a few two-cylinder types survive, such as this handsome 11B Class 2–8–0—and what a distinctly Scottish aura she has! One hundred of these engines once worked the 5 ft 6 in gauge lines of the pampa. This picture reveals the decline of a once magnificent railway. The work-weary 11B, begrimed and ailing, sits in the decaying depot at Olavarria, while the main lines outside see but a fraction of their former traffic.

58 An inside-cylinder 0–6–0—the trusty maid of all work on
Britain's railways for over a century—shrouded in fire, smoke and
steam during a rainy night at Malakwal Junction in the Punjab.
Building of this form of locomotive began in the 1830s and
continued into the 1940s. Tens of thousands—embracing scores
of different designs—ran the length and breadth of Britain. Some
classes were built in enormous numbers, such as the London and
North Western Railway's Ramsbottom DX, which totalled 943
engines. Though most frequently employed upon loose-coupled
freights, the 0–6–0 often worked passenger trains—especially on
branch and cross-country services. During the later years, their
balanced proportions and moderate size rendered them suitable
for shunting duties, and many gained an extra lease of life in this
role. Many were shipped abroad in export packages, and it is
heartening that some can still be found, albeit only on the Indian
subcontinent.

59

59 Vigorous action at the Indian Iron and Steel Corporation's Burnpur Works in Bengal as a giant ladle is filled with molten iron. The locomotive is a 2–6–0 tank engine built by Nasmyth Wilson of Patricroft, Manchester, and one of a fleet of 30 which once worked the 5 ft 6 in gauge lines of the Bombay Port Trust. Introduced in 1913, these curious engines have outside cylinders and a short wheelbase. Some still survive in Bombay docks.

60

60 Apart from being highly functional, this locomotive is significant historically as the last crane engine left in commercial service. She survives at an Indian sleeper depot, and her job is to carry huge tree trunks into the factory, where they are cut up for use on the main line network. Before the engine arrived in 1903, the work was done by elephants. She is in exactly the same condition as when she was built to the order of the Secretary of State for India by Manning Wardle of Leeds over three-quarters of a century ago. Both the crane structure and the auxiliary engine came from the nearby works of Joseph Booth and Sons, situated in the Leeds suburb of Rodley. This locomotive was the only one of its class to be built, and runs on the Indian Railway's broad gauge of 5 ft 6 in.

61 Argentina's General Roca Railway retained a handful of broad-gauge steam engines into the 1980s, although the surviving classes had been reduced to odd engines. This is the last survivor of the BE Class 0–6–0 saddle tank, first introduced by North British in 1904 and subsequently built by Kerr Stuart and Co. of Stoke-upon-Trent. These BEs were a standard shunting engine for Argentina's 5 ft 6 in gauge railways. This last example is seen inside the shed at Bahía Blanca—one of the last havens of the country's broad-gauge steam. The BEs have a delightfully Scottish look about them. Superficially, they appear to be a larger version of the Caledonian railway's celebrated four-coupled Pugs. It was inevitable that private builders should produce designs akin to those on Britain's main line railways—albeit at times subconsciously.

'spinning her 6 ft 2 in driving wheels
at 60 miles an hour'

62 The inside-cylinder 4–4–0 was the principal express passenger type of late Victorian and Edwardian Britain. Similar engines to those used at home were shipped abroad, and today the last examples of this great dynasty are ending their days working cross-country passenger trains over the Punjab of Pakistan. Classified SPS by Pakistan Railways, they were first built by Beyer Peacock in 1904 as part of the British Engineering Standard Committee's 1903 plan to reduce the plethora of designs demanded by the independent railway companies of India. Two designs were initially produced for the broad gauge: the 4–4–0 under discussion and, for goods trains, an inside-cylinder 0–6–0 with an identical boiler. Several famous British chief mechanical engineers were involved in this scheme. Seventy-five years later these SPSs can still spin their 6 ft 2 in diameter driving wheels at speeds of 60 miles an hour. The SPSs are, in essence, a typical Manchester locomotive, being rather similar to the Manchester, Sheffield and Lincolnshire Railway's 4–4–0s designed a few years previously by Henry Pollitt. The MSLR's works were at Gorton and located immediately opposite those of Beyer Peacock. The company's main line ran between, and the two works were connected by an overbridge. These 4–4–0s vividly remind one of the Victorian steam express in its heyday.

62

THE
NORTH AMERICAN
SCHOOL

America's first locomotives came from Britain, but home building began early. One of the first home-built engines was Matthias Baldwin's 'Old Ironsides' of 1832, a 2–2–0 based on the Planet Class from Robert Stephenson's Newcastle works. The many difficulties encountered with this engine caused Mr Baldwin to remark 'this is our last locomotive'. Fortunately, he rescinded this decision, and over the following 123 years the great Philadelphia company which Matthias Baldwin founded was to build some 70,000 locomotives.

Within four years of 'Old Ironsides' being steamed in 1832, evolution had produced the first of what was to become a definitive American locomotive—the 4–4–0. This type suited the country's early railroads, which were built cheaply. The country was new and thinly populated; traffic was sparse; and the hurriedly built lines spanning long distances were constructed of light rails. Under these conditions, speed was neither practical nor particularly necessary—after all, an average of 15 miles an hour was faster than any horse, stagecoach or riverboat! The 4–4–0 provided exactly the right combination of power and tracking, and it remained predominant until the 1870s.

The flamboyance of these 4–4–0s has become part of American folklore; their sensuous form—unhampered by loading gauge restrictions—was to become as classically American as Huckleberry Finn. Ornate headlamps, spark-averting smokestacks, brass bells, cowcatchers, fluted domes and rounded outside cylinders were hallmarks as, with smoke belching from their stacks, they rolled across the New World to open up the interior to unprecedented levels of trade.

America's locomotive development was destined to lead the world, and in 1847 the coal-hauling Philadelphia and Reading Railroad acquired a 4–6–0, thus achieving 50 per cent more power. By 1863 the 2–6–0 had appeared; known as the Mogul, it proved ideal for mixed-traffic work, as the leading pony trucked adequately on the better trackbeds. Moguls became widely used for both home and export and never left the maker's catalogues.

The busy coal lines of the east, however, constantly needed greater power to move bigger tonnages—especially over the Alleghenies—and during the 1860s the 2–8–0, or Consolidation, appeared. Engines of this type opened up possibilities for much longer freight trains and remained predominant upon such duties until the turn of the century. However, this was progress achieved at a cost; the Consolidation demanded heavier rail, better bridges, better wagons and air-brakes, in addition to longer turntables and passing loops as well as improved shunting yard trackage. Once these improvements were carried out, the country's commensurate upsurge as an industrial power demanded that the locomotive designers go all out for bigger and better motive power. An indication of this striving is given by the development of the 4–8–0 and even ten-coupled traction during the 1880s—albeit in small numbers.

A locomotive's power is dictated by its boiler and firebox. All engines mentioned so far had their fireboxes either between the coupled wheels or above them, which limited their power output. The introduction of the 2–4–2 Columbia type overcame this disadvantage. Designed for fast passenger work on upgraded tracks, the Columbia had 7 ft 0 in diameter driving wheels and its trailing axle permitted of the use of a wide firebox.

Poor tracking stability rendered the Columbia precarious. The addition of a four-wheeled truck created the Atlantic 4–4–2, which appeared during the 1890s for the Atlantic City Railroad and 50 mile sprints during which the average speed was in excess of 70 miles an hour were achieved with trains of six cars. The scene was now set for the advent of the Pacific 4–6–2, which combined the power of a 4–6–0—which by this time had widely replaced the 4–4–0—with the qualities of an Atlantic. Purely a 20th century concept, the mainline Pacific with a wide grate appeared in 1902, and by 1910 had become the principal form of express passenger locomotive in America, some 7,000 eventually being built.

Once the principle of the wide firebox was established, the Mogul developed into the 2–6–2 Prairie type and many variations were made on this theme. Events progressed rapidly: the quest for more speed and power led to the eight-coupled locomotive with wide firebox and around the turn of the century the Mikado was born out of a marriage between the 2–8–0 and 2–6–2. As freights became faster and heavier, the Mikado assumed great importance and 14,000 were built for domestic service. It was among the last steam types to disappear and featured extensively in exports for over half a century. The Mikado's debut was somewhat eclipsed by the simultaneous introduction of the 2–10–2 Santa Fé, which provided an enormous power potential along with an even distribution of weight on the track.

Incredible as these advances on the conventional engine were, they became overshadowed by an event which occurred at the World Fair in St Louis in 1904, when the Baltimore and Ohio exhibited 'Old Maude'—a semi-articulated 0–6–6–0 four-cylinder compound Mallet. She was the largest and most powerful locomotive in the world and had a tractive effort of 71,500 lb. 'Maude' appeared complete with outside Walschaerts valve gear, a feature which soon spread to other designs. The engine had no leading trucks, as it was intended for banking duties, but it did provide a blueprint for the ultimate in American steam traction; by 1906 a 2–6–6–2 had appeared. The Great Northern and Western roads found the Mallet ideal to combat the Rockies and by 1912 a tractive effort of 115,000 lb had been achieved with a 2–8–8–2, the prevailing philosophy of the day being low speeds but vast tonnages per train.

Thus, between 1895 and the advent of World War I, American motive power had undergone a complete metamorphosis.

Thenceforth the 4–4–0, 2–6–0 and 2–6–2 ceased to play any important role, and by 1910 the advent of all-steel passengers cars ended the Atlantic's pre-eminence. In terms of freight operation, 2–10–2s proved faster on straight-track hauls, whereas the slower Mallet was ideal wherever grades and curves abounded. For more lively operations the Mikado was preferred, as the big cylinders and small wheels of the Santa Fé were unsuited to running at speed.

It will be seen that America was the trend-setter in the evolution of locomotive types; Pacifics were in general use when the 4–4–0 was at its zenith in Britain, while America aspired to the main-line Mallet around the time Britain introduced the 2–8–0.

From 1905 the vast majority of America's locomotive building—for both home and export—was undertaken by the 'big three': Baldwins of Philadelphia; The American Locomotive Company (Alco) of Schenectady in New York State; and Lima of Ohio. Alco, who also had works in Montreal, was formed in 1901 to match the capacity of Baldwins and it incorporated many famous names of the 19th century such as Rogers and Cooke. The 'big three'— along with their subsidiaries—built the overwhelming majority of the amazing total of some 180,000 American-built locomotives; literally thousands of different classes were represented in this massive output.

Unlike Britain, the railway companies, though private, built few locomotives, the 'big three' being the precursors in design policy in conjunction with the mechanical engineers of the various railroads. This system gave rise to easy communications and a high degree of standardization, which facilitated rapid delivery at competitive prices. In their later years Baldwins were capable of producing twelve giant locomotives a day! Ultimate standardization, however, was anathema to the American way of thinking, and individualism among the railroads prevailed throughout.

The history of the American steam locomotive is generally one of simplicity. It was less sophisticated in outline than most of its counterparts around the world but was built robustly to a moderate economy. The prerequisites were a fine steaming capacity and an ability to work reliably over long distances with a minimum of maintenance. Inside-cylinder engines had no place; a few were built during the early years but outside cylinders soon became adopted as standard. Simple traction predominated throughout, but one notable exception was the Mallet, which appeared in both simple and compound form after it was found that, for slow slugging hauling at full throttle, multi-expansion did show economies.

During the early years of locomotive manufacture, no suitable facilities existed for producing plate frames and the bar principle was adopted instead. This was found ideal and the system was retained. The cylinders and boiler saddle were cast in two units and bolted together down the centre, which resulted in the familiar stays from smokebox saddle to front framing.

From the outset, high running-plates provided accessibility to moving parts. During the later years, however, labour saving, ease of maintenance and high utilization became something of a science and led to the adoption of such sophistications as roller bearings, self-cleaning smokeboxes, rocking grates, mechanical stokers and the bar frame's derivative the cast steel bed, which was a locomotive backbone in one casting comprising cylinders, smokebox saddle, side frames and cross-stretcher.

Typical American engines were exported all over the world and a widespread adoption of their characteristics ensued. Among the countries with a large percentage of American-type engines—the result of either physical imports or design influence—were Canada, Mexico and Central America, Cuba, Brazil, South Africa, Australia,

Russia, China and, in the last years of steam building, India also. The export of special war engines also promoted transatlantic thinking, and one remembers the Pershing 2–8–0 of World War I and the S160 2–8–0s of World War II—among many others.

Another milestone in development occurred in 1911, when the 4–8–2 Mountain type came into general use. In one sense, this was an upgraded 2–8–2 with better tracking facilities, but it could also be regarded as an extension of the Pacific. The Mountain proved to be an ideal mixed-traffic type and, in common with its Mikado antecedent, was to have a far-reaching effect on world locomotive practice—in addition to being a predominant export type.

The insatiable demand for tractive effort burst through new barriers with the adoption of a four-wheel trailer truck, which allowed for bigger boilers and fireboxes, and in 1925 Lima produced a 2–8–4 known as the Berkshire. This heralded a new generation of superpower and set the pattern for the final stages of steam development. If the Berkshire added potency to the Mikado, then a 2–10–4 was a logical extension of the Santa Fé. The first was built by Lima in 1926 for the Texas and Pacific Railroad. Known as the Texas type, it was an important advancement on earlier ten-coupled designs, whose firebox capacities were limited by overhang. The Texas was built in small-wheel and large-wheel versions—some of up to 6 ft 2 in diameter—and was the supreme American superpower, its superior tracking ability enabling it to supersede the Santa Fé.

The advent of 4–6–4 Hudsons and 4–8–4 Confederations was a natural progression, and marvellous working ability and smooth riding were combined with pleasing engine proportions. Thus, by 1930 almost all the ingredients had evolved to carry America's steam locomotive to its ultimate development.

Magnificent as these events were, there were equally impressive achievements during the streamlined era of the 1930s when the specially built high-speed Atlantics on the Chicago, Milwaukee, St Paul and Pacific Railroad worked the Hiawatha Express over its 431 mile run from Chicago to Milwaukee in 400 minutes, including intermediate station stops. To achieve this, sustained speeds of over 100 miles an hour were necessary. Furthermore, it will be remembered that a Pennsylvania Atlantic allegedly achieved 127 miles an hour.

The ultimate development, however, centred upon the Mallet, which by this time was also built as a four-cylinder simple. Improved design eliminated previous speed restrictions and ensured faster running. Indeed, the 6,000 horse-power 4–6–6–4 Challengers, built between 1936 and 1944, were capable of speeds in excess of 60 miles an hour. These titans weighed 300 tons and could consume 18 tons of coal per hour!

'The Great American Railroad Show', as it has been called, was moving towards its climax and in 1944 this was reached when the Union Pacific built the 25 7,000 horse-power 4–8–8–4 'Big Boys', the largest steam locomotives of all time. This giant of giants had a grate area of 150 square feet and packed its punches with an incredible tractive effort of 135,400 lb. The 'Big Boys' are truly unforgettable and they survived until 1958. During those last years the Union Pacific provided a fabulous hunting ground for enthusiasts, as the Big Boys could be seen in company with Challengers and 4–12–2s.

Evolution could go no further; the ultimate capacity had seemingly been reached, but not before the steam locomotive had helped build up America to be the greatest nation on earth. No greater contrast exists in railway history than that between Matthias Baldwin's 5 ton 'Old Ironsides' of 1831 and the 520 ton 'Big Boys' of little over a century later.

63 A dramatic study of semi-streamlined WP Pacifics, made at Lucknow shed in northern India, which reveals something of the marvellous atmosphere of a main line steam depot. The thrill of watching big Pacifics being prepared for working long-distance trains is nowadays tempered by the uneasy knowledge that such sights will soon become a part of history.

64 It used to be a common practice among British railway enthusiasts to look down upon modern utilitarian designs which were built in large numbers to replace older and more interesting classes. These Indian broad-gauge 2–8–2s could be similarly disdained. Originally supplied to cope with the enormous increase in traffic on Indian railways during World War II, they have since become a standard all-round design. Typically American, some 800 were delivered between 1943 and 1949 and they have taken the classification AWD and CWD—the former referring to American-built engines, the latter to Canadian-built. The type can be seen right across the Indian subcontinent from Pakistan to Bangladesh. In India they play second fiddle to the larger WG 2–8–2s. The two classes between them almost monopolize freight, shunting and pilot duties. This picture was made at Chitpur depot, just outside Calcutta, where some 45 AWD/CWDs are allocated.

63

64

'some sort of mechanization is vital'

65 British enthusiasts were used to seeing the principal locomotive sheds equipped with mechanical coaling plants, but these were few and far between around the world. At many Indian depots coaling is done manually with wicker baskets by means of a ladder perched against the engine's tender. At the larger sheds, however, some sort of mechanization is vital. This picture, from the Howrah steam sheds in Calcutta, depicts a mobile steam coaling-crane in action. These highly personable machines have a vertical boiler and move freely around the coaling area. Labourers manually load the 1 ton buckets—18 of which are needed to fill the tender of this WP Pacific. The crane was built in Britain by James Booth and Bros., of Rodley in Leeds, while the Pacific came from the Chittaranjan locomotive works in West Bengal in 1964.

65

67

66 One example of the imaginative embellishments applied to India's semi-streamlined WP Pacifics. A detailed study of these adornments would be fascinating, different regions and even individual depots being noted for their particular styling. Although India's steam locomotives are predominantly black, their colourful lining out—combined with these embellishments—renders them delightful to behold. Unfortunately, few engines are actually named, but when the WPs work a famous express, they invariably carry its headboard above the front buffer beam. These Indian WPs are particularly significant as representing the last tangible reminder of the glorious streamlining trend which became fashionable in many parts of the world during the 1930s.

67 The sugar plantations of Campos State in Brazil constitute one of the finest hunting grounds for steam traction today. Here many former main line engines of metre gauge remain hard at work during the milling season—as witness this delightful Baldwin 2–8–0, seen out on the Pocogordo Line of the Barcelos Usina. Built in 1894, she remains a splendid engine for such duties, and is caught by the camera speeding towards the factory with a trainload of freshly cut cane. Throughout Brazil, steam locomotives are referred to as 'Maria Fumacas'; translated, this means 'Smoke Marys'—a name which seems to suit these American-styled engines to perfection.

68

68   The Indian railways looked towards American design practice when, following World War II, a new standard express passenger locomotive was required for the broad gauge. After consultations with Baldwins during the mid-1940s, a new design was prepared in accordance with specific Indian requirements. The result was the WP, and the first batch arrived from Baldwins in 1947. They proved to be very spirited performers, and although the driving wheel diameter of 5 ft 7 in seems small for a mail and express passenger engine, sustained speeds of over 60 miles an hour were easily possible, which was adequate for Indian conditions. Their axle loading is only 18½ tons, and this gives them an excellent route availability. Building continued until 1967, by which time a grand total of 755 had been reached, with engines having been built in Canada, Poland, Austria and, not least, at India's Chittaranjan locomotive works in West Bengal. No WPs were built in Britain—a marked contrast with India's past locomotive traditions. The WPs—which were partly conceived to avoid certain deficiencies inherent in the earlier British Pacifics—have lived up to all expectations. The vast majority are still active and many will continue to undertake important services throughout the 1980s. This class—along with their relations the WG 2–8–2s—will go down in history as one of the most significant locomotive types of all time. The picture shows one snaking past the camera at over 60 miles an hour with a heavy express on the South Central Railway.

'the big Mallet was even more fabulous than I had imagined'

70

69 One of Latin America's most exciting railways is the 2 ft 6 in gauge network centred upon São João del Rei in the Brazilian state of Minas Gerais. The system has a stable of vintage Baldwins consisting of 4–4–0s, 4–6–0s and 2–8–0s, the oldest dating from 1889 and the most recent from 1920. All are oil burners. Here No. 37—a 4–6–0 of 1911—waits in a crossing loop during a violent tropical downpour in the early hours of the morning. Worked entirely by steam, the system represents US-style railroading of the 1890s faithfully maintained by the local repair shops, who, with great ingenuity, manufacture most of the replacement parts for the locomotives and wooden rolling stock. It is truly amazing how these old and ostensibly obsolete engines engender feelings of pride—punctuality and cleanliness being of prime concern.

70 A long-standing wish was fulfilled when I finally encountered this freakish four-cylinder compound 0–6–6–0 Baldwin Mallet hauling mahogany for the Insular Lumber Company on the Philippine island Negros. As with many of the engines that I have waited a long time to see, No. 7—as the big Mallet was called— was even more fabulous than I had imagined. It was dark when I first saw her, as she clanked by with a string of log cars, mahogany sparks curling off her smokestack and grotesque sounds emanating from her four leaking cylinders. This engine's duty was to convey freshly cut logs from the mountain stands down to the sawmill situated at coast level; the journey was precarious and derailments frequent. The picture shows the engine beginning her journey and easing onto the wooden trestle viaduct at Maaslud. Tragically, the Insular Lumber Company have now closed this line and No. 7 lies abandoned.

71

71   The first of these American-built I5CA Class 4–8–2s arrived in South Africa in 1925. Known as 'Big Bills', they proved extremely successful, and, along with their relations the 16D Pacifics, they precipitated a fundamental shift towards American practice in South Africa. Ninety-six were built, and although they came initially from Baldwin and Alco, later batches were obtained from Breda of Milan and North British. The line between Witbank and Pretoria was a fine place to see these historic 4–8–2s in action. The route undulates like corrugated iron and the engines emit a characteristically sharp staccato bark as they attack the grades. The picture was made at Panpoort—a well-known crossing point on this single-track route. The semaphore signals facing the camera are for trains entering the loops from the opposite direction.

72   A high-stepping chocolate-coloured beauty discovered on pilot duties at San Bernardo locomotive works near Santiago. She is of 5 ft 6 in gauge and is the last survivor of the Chilean Railway's once-numerous 38 Class. The engine is distinctive for two reasons. First, she represents the early tradition of ten-wheelers (4–6–0s) in America, which, with their fireboxes placed between the rear two coupled axles, were an extension of the early 4–4–0. Second, she is probably the only remaining engine built by Rogers of New Jersey, having come from their works in 1896. Rogers began building locomotives in 1837 and was responsible for many beautifully styled engines until the firm became absorbed into Alco in 1905. Although relegated to humble tasks, the engine does operate the employees' passenger train between the works and the main line station. At five o'clock each afternoon the big works gates open and with chime whistle echoing the 4–6–0 eases her train of antiquated coaches onto the main line, conjuring up memories of the days when thousands of her sisters rolled across America.

'these last cathedrals of steam'

73 A brace of American-styled Class I5CA 4–8–2 'Big Bills' amid the smoky gloom of the South African Railway's Witbank shed on the Transvaal. The sunlight filters through the blackened windows of the depot and reacts dramatically with the smoke and steam emanating from the engines inside. One can almost smell the soot and the oil, odours which evoke the incredible atmosphere of these last cathedrals of steam.

74 This engine works for the Hawaiian-Philippine Co. on Negros and is known as Dragon No. 6. She is a 3 ft 6 in gauge 0–6–0 with 12 in diameter cylinders, built by Baldwins in 1920. The operating company is noted for its roster of cabbage-stack Baldwins, which, resplendent in their red livery, look more like the contents of a museum line than of a serious railway. The engines maintain a radio contact with the factory control office so that their movements may be co-ordinated throughout the plantation. For most of the season the Hawaiian-Philippine Co.'s engines burn bagasse—the natural waste from sugar cane processing. Though extremely low in calorific value, this waste constitutes a free source of energy and, although two firemen are needed to feed the locomotive constantly, bagasse is preferable to imported higher calorific fuels such as coal, oil or wood. Notice that the engine's enormous tender is piled to the roof with the golden fuel. Upon leaving the factory the first wagon of the rake was also loaded with bagasse, but this has since been consumed, as the train is depicted 10 miles out in the sugar plantation.

75 This short-haul freight on the Teresa Cristina has a Baldwin 2–8–2 of 1946 in charge, known as 'Grimy Hog'. She originally worked on Brazil's Centro Oeste network. 'Hog' is a typical American product, albeit scaled down to metre gauge.

75

76

76 My journey to Usina Barcelos in Campos State, Brazil, was full of anticipation. This sugar factory had a metre-gauge 4–4–0 built by Baldwin in 1876—possibly the last real period American 4–4–0 left in service. Upon arrival, however, a bitter disappointment awaited me: the 4–4–0 was derelict and partly dismembered, having been withdrawn from service two years previously. The journey was not wasted, however, consolation for the disappointment being provided by this beautifully proportioned 2–4–0 which was busily engaged around the factory. Built by Baldwins in 1920, this engine's wheel arrangement is unusual in American practice, as the 2–4–0 is generally associated with 19th century Britain. She provides the strange spectacle of a modern well-proportioned design on an early wheel arrangement and must be one of the few 2–4–0 tender engines in existence. Despite the engine's being maintained in perfect trim, the factory manager stated that withdrawal was imminent—the owner having earmarked her as a static exhibit for the grounds of his house! If this occurs, it would typify the piecemeal but meaningful preservation methods of countries like Brazil.

'animation on the coaling road'

77 Animation on the coaling road at Bandel depot in Bengal, as a Canadian-built CWD Class 2–8–2 is fuelled up by one of the Eastern Railway's ubiquitous steam cranes. The crane, caught easing the 1 ton coal bucket into position, was built by Thomas Smith and Son in Rodley, Leeds. To facilitate this method of coaling, the fuel is unloaded manually from the transit wagons and placed between adjacent tracks on the coaling road. The locomotives requiring coal move onto one track and the crane moves alongside on the other. Labourers fill the bucket manually and the crane swings it up to the fireman, just visible on the engine's tender. The two men in the foreground are engaged in shovelling up the remaining slack as the coal supply diminishes. The jets of steam are from the blow-down valve, a device which ejects scum and chemical impurities from within the engine's boiler and, at full pressure, ejects them into the atmosphere.

78 It is ironic that France, the home of multi-cylinder compounds, should have broken those noble locomotive traditions by taking in 1,323 of these rugged American 2–8–2s. However, so great was the damage inflicted upon France's railways during World War II—as a result of either the German invasion or acts of sabotage during the occupation, or when the enemy retreated— that only a small part of the system remained intact. From a total of 17,000 locomotives, only 3,000 were operable; new motive power was desperately needed. Accordingly, the American and Canadian builders, with their mass production techniques, responded with the postwar delivery of these 141 Rs—or 'Liberations', as the new Mikados were popularly called. Readily utilized and very free-steaming, they were a great success. The class formed an effective backbone for French steam traction, and as late as 1970 could still be found hauling the Golden Arrow express between Calais and Amiens. The 141 Rs outlived all the indigenous French designs to become the country's last steam locomotives. The picture shows one heading away under the electrification catenary at Narbonne.

79

79 The MacArthur 2–8–2 is one of the most celebrated war engines of all time. Introduced during World War II for the United States Army Transportation Corps' operations in the Far East, the type saw extensive service on the metre-gauge networks of India, Burma, Malaya, Thailand and the Philippines. All were built in America—the majority during the crucial years 1942 to 1944—though some were completed after the war. In true American fashion, they were eager steamers and popular with their crews. Classified MAWD, many remain hard at work in various parts of India, especially in the North East Frontier Railways—the latter system embracing Assam, where the type is particularly revered. The illustration shows one complete with typical Indian embellishments at the huge steam sheds at Garakphur.

80 One of the Turkish State Railway's 'Skyliner' 2–10–0s. The fascination here is the essence of the watering procedure, and the way in which the engine resembles a mighty beast. Eighty-eight of these powerful decapods were sent to Turkey in 1947–9 from the Vulcan Iron Works in Pennsylvania.

81

81   This curve, situated to the north of Bloemfontein in the Orange Free State, was once the most famous railway photographic spot in South Africa. It is located on a 9 mile climb at 1 in 100, and on busy days during the early 1970s over 100 steam trains would pass—many of them double-headed. The track at this point is overlooked by a tall koppie, and photographers armed with long lenses would congregate at various elevations and shoot the endless succession of trains climbing northwards from Bloemfontein. The hillside afforded a panoramic view of the surrounding veld, and on clear frosty mornings, when the exhausts rose high into the air, it was possible to count up to seven trains approaching at different intervals from the south. Such a situation was almost too good to be true, and by 1975 the location had been marred by the erection of electrification catenary. The picture shows a South African Railways standard 23 Class 4–8–2—German-built in 1938—passing the celebrated koppie with a sixteen-coach special bound for Kroonstad.

82   Ever since I heard of the existence in Brazil of this unusual 2–6–2 saddle tank, I had an ambition to include her in a future book. My information—albeit several years out of date—stated that the engine shunted around the workshops at Lavras and was Baldwin Extra Order No. 372 of 1927. Lavras lies many miles from the coast in the state of Minas Gerais, Brazil, and before making the journey I tried to find out from official sources in Rio whether the engine still existed. Unbelievably, no one could provide any information; the only solution was to go and see for myself. The engine indeed existed—and in the resplendent condition shown. Known as the 'Lavras Rose', the engine is here depicted against a backdrop of banana groves.

82

83

84

83 In the middle of nowhere, in the middle of the night, a wood-burning Baldwin 2–8–0 of 1890s vintage wheezes its way up a steep gradient with a trainload of sugar bound for Conceição de Macabu Usina in Campos State, Brazil. Scenes such as this would attract thousands of tourists in many parts of the world, but in Brazil this is vintage railroading played for real and hard dollar-earning business, sugar being an important part of the national economy. By night, these sugar plantations have a wild beauty: the black sky reveals stars of a Van Gogh-like clarity mocked by innumerable fireflys and far away the glow of a blazing cane field flickers in the sky, adding piquancy to an atmosphere laced by whistles and barks from distant locomotives.

84 This type of engine was the brainchild of Ephraim Shay, a backwoods logging engineer who required a locomotive to haul heavy lumber trains over temporary tracks frequently engulfed in mud and abounding in curves and gradients. The conventional locomotive would have been too rigid, too heavy and unable to grip the rails. Shay's engine had its wheels mounted in articulated trucks which, apart from providing flexibility, spread out the weight. Vertical cylinders—placed on the engine's right-hand side—drove a horizontal shaft which was connected to all wheels by means of pinions slotted into bevelled gears. The crankshaft was made flexible by incorporating universal joints. This geared transmission provided an easy turning movement and enabled the engines to work under adverse conditions. Two-, three- and even four-truck variants were built. As the cylinders were set on the right, the boiler was correspondingly offset to the left. The Shay was adopted by Lima of Ohio, with whom it is associated in the same way that its articulated relation, the Garratt, is associated with Beyer Peacock of Manchester. The engine shown is a two-truck, three-cylinder example working for the Insular Lumber Company in the Philippines.

85

85 Many enthusiasts regard the Teresa Cristina Railway in Brazil as being one of the last real railways on earth. Operated entirely by steam, the line boasts powerful 2–10–4s with 70 square foot grate areas. These giants pull loads of 1,800 tons at top speeds in excess of 60 miles an hour—abundant evidence that the system is still a monument to American steam superpower. This immaculate and efficiently run railway is enduring proof of the magnificent job which can be done by steam in an age when it is fashionable to deride it as an outmoded form of technology. The team spirit and pride in the job felt throughout the Teresa Cristina is in the very best of steam railway traditions, for the network has never known the debilitating effect of dieselization. The photographer can simply set up his camera by the trackside and photograph the endless procession of trains as they roar along between the mines west of Tubarão and the docks at Imbituba.

86 A delightful engine lovingly prepared for one of the famous locomotive beauty contests held in New Delhi. She is the exhibit for the Eastern Railway and is seen leaving her home depot at Asansol in Bengal prior to running to New Delhi for the judging. In this particular contest each region of the Indian Railways system was requested to submit a WP suitably decked in different colours and further embellished with ornaments. The Indians have a flair for such beautification and some startling exhibits resulted. Apart from the tremendous interest they create, these competitions help to engender feelings of pride and a concern for cleanliness throughout the system.

स्वयंवर

7247   W P

'the yard is crammed
with vibrant, hissing silhouettes'

87 The unforgettable atmosphere of a big steam shed is conjured up in this scene at Tubarão in Brazil. The yard is crammed with vibrant, hissing silhouettes which must be kept hot in readiness for the new week's workings. A small team of steam raisers flit from engine to engine to tend the fires and keep the boilers topped up with water, for the steam locomotive—unlike the diesel—needs to be kept hot and ready, and maintaining it in light steam throughout the day of rest is more economical than dropping the fire completely.

87

88 A vertical-cylinder Shay, a bizarre machine which flits through the jungles at the dead of night and sprays the tropical vegetation with fire. Old Shay No. 12 was built by Lima of Ohio early this century and works for the Insular Lumber Company on the Philippine island of Negros. With huge cylindrical chimney, circular off-pitch boiler and wooden rectangular buffer beam, these weird locomotives, which came rumbling out of the American backwoods, represent the ultimate in romantic fantasy with a modern colour camera.

89 Having taken its refreshment, a mighty Texas type 2–10–4 from the Teresa Cristina line in Brazil sidles away into the smoky haze of its depot in the background; meanwhile, in the foreground, the water column drips noisily.

90 Classic British and American war engines stand side by side in this historic scene from a locomotive graveyard in Greece. On the left is one of the celebrated War Department 2–10–0s, the first engines of this wheel arrangement to appear in Britain. They were introduced in 1943 as a light axle-weight variant of the more numerous War Department 2–8–0 and caused widespread interest at the time of their inception. When these 2–10–0s appeared in Britain, the type had long been established in Europe and America. Although the last disappeared from Britain in 1962, a few were destined to remain at work in Greece and Syria until the mid-1970s. The engine's companion is one of Major Marsh's S160 2–8–0s of World War II.

89

90

91

91 The run-down of main-line steam all over the world has meant that in many countries the surviving locomotives are often relegated to either shunting or short-haul duties on secondary lines. India and China provide obvious exceptions, as, to a lesser degree, does South Africa, with such busy lines as the veritable racetrack between Kimberley and De Aar. This route remains primarily worked by the 23 Class 4–8–2s and the larger 25NC Class 4–8–4s—the noncondensing sisters of the celebrated 25s discussed in the caption to Plate 113. Speeds on this line are often well in excess of 60 miles an hour, despite the 3 ft 6 in gauge. Here a brace of 23s bounds along with a heavy freight. Tremendous pride exists on the line, many engines being ceremoniously named by their crews. All trains stop for water and fire-raking at Orange River, and it is common to see crews vigorously polishing their already spotless locomotives. Much of this pride stems from the inspiration provided by that great railwayman the late Gordon Watson, who was shed foreman at De Aar for many years.

92 Engine No. 7—a Baldwin 2–8–0 of 1894—storms out of a loading siding with a heavy rake of sugar cane. The engine—which began life in the 1890s on the metre-gauge Leopoldina Railway—is seen working for Usina Outeiro in Campos State, Brazil. No. 7 has bar frames, each of her cylinders is cast with half of the smokebox saddle—as witness the protruding stays—and the cylinders are topped with rectangular valve chests. Her boiler sports a stovepipe chimney, followed by the sand dome—the steam dome being placed towards the firebox. These features contrast with those of the pure British locomotive of the same period, which was built with plate frames, cylinders cast separately without support stays or visible valve chest, a styled chimney with rim, steam dome placed centrally on the boiler, and sand carried elsewhere on the engine. Comparisons may be made with some of the British engines—albeit slightly hybridized ones—on Plates 32 and 58.

93 Their day's duty done, three Baldwin-built giants congregate in the shed yard at Tubarão on the Teresa Cristina line. On the right is one of the line's three surviving 2–6–6–2 Mallets, built in 1950, standing in front of a 1946-built 2–8–2. This latter engine—known as 'Grimy Hog'—is the only one of its type on the line. On the left is a Texas 2–10–4 of 1940. This coal-carrying system is located in southeastern Brazil and runs from inland mines to the docks at Imbituba. Not all the coal is exported, as large tonnages are now delivered to the giant Capivari power station, located near Tubarão. Main-line hauls are undertaken by the line's roster of fourteen 2–10–4s; 'Grimy Hog' acts as pilot engine around Tubarão, while the Mallet is little more than a standby. The Teresa Cristina operates predominantly by daylight, and at dawn the first trainloads of empties leave Tubarão bound for the various mines. The locomotives return with loads from late morning onwards, and by mid-evening the majority of the engines are back on shed.

'Baldwin-built giants congregate in the shed yard'

95

94 The increase in transportation during World War II was of such magnitude that special engines were hastily designed for the purpose and often built in enormous numbers. Many war engines are included among the most famous locomotive designs, and one—the Hunslet Austerity 0–6–0 saddle tank—has become the most numerous preserved steam class in the world. The engine shown here, clumsily taking water in northern Greece, is of a classic wartime design built in America for the United States Army Transportation Corps. These standard-gauge 0–6–0 tank engines were used for shunting in army depots and port areas as well as for general back-up duties behind the advancing Allied armies, and were in many ways the American equivalent of the British Hunslet Austerity. The class numbered several hundred strong and all came from the lesser-known American builders H. K. Porter, Vulcan Ironworks and Davenport Locomotive Works. British enthusiasts associate them with Southampton Docks, where 14 were employed until the early 1960s.

95 A classic American switcher—or shunting engine in English parlance—at a steel foundry in Brazil. What a fine backdrop the works makes for an engine whose shape recalls the cartoons of Rowland Emett. In the background an overhead crane conveys a huge cauldron containing molten steel. Within minutes the steel will be tipped into moulds to form ingots and the engine will convey these, still red-hot and flaming, round to the rolling mill. To watch this amazing engine pulling its load of ingots against a fiery backdrop of discharging furnaces is unforgettable; dense clouds of smoke issue from the locomotive's chimney, flaming cinders bounce along the tracksides, while its whistle blares like an anguished banshee above the clamour of the works. Built by Baldwins in November 1896, this 5 ft 6 in gauge 0–6–2 saddle tank worked on Brazil's Paulista Railway until 1944, when it was sold to the present owners. Past the blazing furnaces, down beyond the smouldering coke-ovens into the stockyard and up to the connection with the main line—all part of the little veteran's everyday chores.

'a nifty little thing
on narrow-gauge tracks'

96

96 However well researched my expeditions in search of locomotives may be, surprises inevitably occur. Often these unexpected finds are the result of chance remarks about an old engine shunting at a remote location. Such was the case with this engine at the Eastern Province Cement Company in Port Elizabeth, South Africa. A stranger had told us to go up to the factory to see what he described as 'a nifty little thing on narrow gauge tracks'. The gateman confirmed that a 2 ft 0 in gauge engine was used by the company, but could give no details and, as the engine was down at the exchange siding with the main line, it was suggested that I await its return. Darkness had fallen before the engine arrived, but imagine how excited I was to be confronted by this red-liveried Baldwin Pacific of 1930. Here was an engine not to be missed—especially as the crew informed me that a new diesel was on order and the engine's withdrawal imminent. At the time no one imagined that the engine would be purchased for preservation and exported to Britain, but today the little Baldwin resides on the Brecon Mount Railway in Powys. This company is building a new 2 ft 0 in gauge track over a 5½ mile section of the former Brecon and Merthyr Railway. When this exciting project is finally completed, it is hoped that the Baldwin will begin a new lease of life hauling passengers through the spectacular scenery of the Brecon Beacons.

97 A Texas 2–10–4, resplendent after receiving a major overhaul, on the Teresa Cristina line in Santa Catarina Province, Brazil. This railway has become a last haven for American steam superpower; the network is completely isolated from the remainder of Brazil's railway system, and is complete with its own locomotive workshops. 2–10–4s monopolize much of the line traffic, but during the late 1970s some additional locomotives were needed following an increase in output from the mines. It was fervently hoped that some of the redundant 59 Class 'Mountain' Garratts might be purchased from the Kenya Railways. Serious consideration was given to the proposal, but in the event the 'Mountain's' 21 ton axle weight proved too high, and it now appears that some 2–10–2 Santa Fés will be obtained from the Belgrano Railway in neighbouring Argentina. This influx of new locomotives does support a general belief that the Teresa Cristina will continue to be 100 per cent steam-worked for some years to come, and with its frequency of traffic and variety of power, it remains a must for all who revere the sight, sound, smell and atmosphere of a real steam railway.

98

98 A Baldwin 4–6–0 T at a factory in India. Built for Britain's 60 cm gauge lines during World War I, the type was intended to supplement the standard Hunslet 4–6–0 T of 1915, and Baldwins built the amazing total of 495 between March 1916 and April 1917. They proved to be less popular than the Hunslets, as, apart from rough riding, they showed a tendency to derail. This resulted in Alco introducing a 2–6–2 T variant, also for British war service, and these engines were an infinitely better proposition, although the two types looked very similar. These three designs formed the Allied equivalent of the 60 cm gauge German 'Feldbahn' 0–8–0 T, of which several thousand were built to a basic design. It is believed that at least 50 of these Baldwin 4–6–0 Ts were sent to India for industrial service following the war's end, and a few remain active today at various sugar factories. The engine shown is Baldwin No. 45380, built for the War Department in 1917.

100

99 Tunnels with their dank, sooty atmosphere are full of mystery and the one at Sideropolis on the Rio Florita branch of the Teresa Cristina in Brazil is no exception. After the 2–10–4s have pounded their way under the hills, they emerge into the rock cutting amid a cataclysmic blast of smoke and steam. Dramas such as these constitute some of the most thrilling aspects of a steam railway. This engine is No. 313, built by Baldwins in 1940, and sub-shedded out at Pinheirinho for working the local mine traffic.

100 These Teresa Cristina Mallets were introduced for the heavily graded and curving line from Tubarão to Lauro Müller in Brazil. Their operations on this section were curtailed in 1974, when a disastrous flood—caused by the River Tubarão bursting its banks—swept away 80 per cent of the track. So disastrous were the floods that many homes were also washed away and people had to flock to the surrounding hills. The cost of repairing the line was higher than the dwindling reserves of coal at Lauro Müller could justify; the line never opened again and the Mallets became redundant. Nowadays the sole survivor is restricted to standby duty, although we see her here storming along with a heavy train on a sultry grey afternoon. Today, depressing convoys of lorries ply between Lauro Müller and Tubarão, while the omnibuses inevitably evoke memories of the three Baldwin Pacifics which once operated the line's passenger service. Only one Pacific survives, and as she trips around Tubarão, she adds further distinction to this railway's fascinating stable of motive power.

'the Brontosaurus of steam'

101 Sadly, the giant Mallet—the Brontosaurus of steam—is virtually extinct. However, a few very active examples can still be found on certain smaller-gauge systems around the world. The engine shown is an excellent example; she is No. 204, one of six metre-gauge 2–6–6–2s, built between 1941 and 1949 by Baldwins for Brazil's Teresa Cristina Railway. Although the traditional Mallet was a four-cylinder compound with large low-pressure cylinders placed at the front, many simples were also built, and No. 204 may be the last of these to survive in main-line service. As the simple Mallet nears extinction on the Teresa Cristina, a stable of compounds survives at Tjibatu in Java, where huge 2–6–6–0s and even larger 2–8–8–0s perform on 3 ft 6 in gauge tracks. Occasionally, the tender Mallets double-head over the hilly routes radiating from Tjibatu and can be seen storming along against a backdrop of volcanic hills—a memorable way to play out the great Mallet tradition.

103

102   Another shot of Usina Outeiro's Baldwin 2–8–0 No. 7 of 1894, emphasizing further some of the distinguishing features enumerated in the caption to Plate 92. Note also the wooden cab complete with louvred windows. It incorporates a front door which opens onto a running plate raised up above the driving wheels. The characteristic British engine of the period has low footplating, possibly with splashers, and a metal cab.

103   The South African Railway's 3 ft 6 in gauge line between Kroonstad and Bloemfontein was until the mid-1970s popularly regarded as the busiest steam-worked route in the world. It became a haven for the ever-increasing bands of globe-trotting enthusiasts anxious to witness the glories of an all-steam main line. The route was worked almost exclusively by the American-influenced 4–8–2 Classes 15F and 23. These standards are direct descendants of the 15CA 4–8–2s known as 'Big Bills', first supplied to South Africa from America in 1925 and discussed in the caption to Plate 71. Here a 23 Class engine departs from Vetrivier—an important watering and fire-raking stop, situated halfway between Kroonstad and Bloemfontein. Stops for fire-raking are unknown in many countries, but in South Africa engines work extremely hard on coal, which tends to clog up. An indication of the care lavished on this graded route is given by the foot-thick layer of cinders by the trackside: even 40 feet back these still measured several inches deep. Furthermore, it was estimated that 1,400 tons of ash was shovelled out of Vetrivier's pits each month. The SAR had a total of 136 Class 23s, all built in Germany between 1938 and 1939. They have 24 inch diameter cylinders, a boiler pressure of 225 pounds per square inch, a 63 square foot grate area, and a coal and water carrying capacity of 18 tons and 9,500 gallons, respectively. In full working order the locomotive and tender weigh 220 tons.

OTHER
EUROPEAN SCHOOLS

Following Britain's lead, railways spread rapidly among the developed nations of Europe. British locomotives were initially supplied in most cases but eventually there emerged various schools of design conceived and produced in the home country, initially for domestic purposes but later for export also. The characteristics of these schools can still be seen amid the dwindling ranks of world steam; a brief review of them will help put the European locomotives illustrated throughout this book into perspective. The German, French and Austrian schools exerted the greatest influence upon world practice, such countries as Italy, Holland, Switzerland, Finland and Spain having distinctive but largely derivative designs.

Germany was the most prolific European exporter of locomotives and products from her builders can still be found in abundance. During the 19th century the various state railways supported by their respective locomotive builders produced a wide range of engines. By far the most important was the Prussian, whose designs were destined to influence both domestic and export policy during the 20th century. Some of the world's most significant steam designs were of Prussian origin, such as the G8 0–8–0 of 1912, the P8 4–6–0 of 1906 and the G12 three-cylinder 2–10–0 of 1915. The G8 and P8 eventually totalled some 5,000 and 3,800 engines, respectively.

Apart from the export market, Germany's engines were also widely distributed as a result of World War I either during the hostilities themselves or in subsequent reparation packages. The creation of modern Poland—parts of which were in Prussia—also meant the inheritance of the previous state's designs.

Shortly after World War I Germany's railways were unified to form the Reichsbahn; and in order to replace the multitude of various designs inherited from the previous administrations—some 300 classes in all—there began a vigorous standardization programme which was to sustain the country's railways until the end of the steam age. The classics among these designs were the 01 Class Pacifics of 1925, the 44 Class three-cylinder 2–10–0s of 1926, the 41 Class 2–8–2s of 1936 and the 50 Class 2–10–0s of 1938. In 1942 this last type was used as the basis for the famous Kriegslokomotive—or war engine—of which some 6,300 were built. Pacifics, Mikados and 2–10–0s between them reached a total of over 13,000 locomotives.

Simple traction was adopted in accordance with latter-day Prussian thinking, and the engines had bar frames, high boilers with short chimneys, large windshields, two domes, boiler-mounted sandboxes and a distinctly cut cab of adequate proportions. The engines were orderly in appearance and satisfying in a rugged and rather angular way, but they never approached the symmetry of British designs. Reichsbahn characteristics occurred whenever German builders prepared export designs, and Poland, Bulgaria, Yugoslavia and Turkey were noted recipients.

The advent of World War II in 1939 precipitated a further spreading of Prussian and Reichsbahn designs resulting from the German occupation of Europe. The Kriegslokomotive predominated, and even in 1980—35 years after the end of the war—it remained at work in Eastern Europe. The Kriegslokomotive and the Prussian G8 are believed to be the second- and third-most numerous steam types in world history. A celebrated German locomotive builder was Henschel of Kassel, a company which has gone down in history as one of the leading locomotive foundries.

Germany is particularly noted for its narrow-gauge industrial and plantation engines and has been a principal exporter of these since the 19th century. The most celebrated industrial builder was Orenstein and Koppel, who had over 13,000 locomotives to their credit; well over half of these were exported for every conceivable type of industrial use. Germany's industrials tended to reflect certain design characteristics of their main-line counterparts; almost all were either side tanks or well tanks and the saddleback—so common in Britain and America—seldom appeared.

Orenstein and Koppel made an important contribution to the industrial locomotive when they pioneered the industrial version of the Fireless. These engines are ideal for shunting in factories with a ready supply of high-pressure steam and are charged through a plug-in valve from the works boilers. One charge enables them to undertake long bouts of shunting before a refill becomes necessary. Apart from its economic advantages, the Fireless is especially valuable for shunting in such environments as munitions and explosive factories or paper mills, where sparks from a conventional engine could have disastrous consequences.

Field military railways were another German speciality, especially during World War I; the celebrated

Feldbahn 600 mm gauge 0–8–0 tank engine was produced by eleven builders and totalled 3,000.

In terms of power and size, French engines tended towards German proportions rather than British. The French school was closely identifiable, as the leading builders supplied only six or seven main-line systems between the middle of the 19th century and 1938, when the national system SNCF was created. The engines produced during the 20th century have an unmistakable outward appearance, with their short cabs, boilers decked with such paraphernalia as feed water heaters, thin-lipped chimneys and domed smokebox doors. The thin piping whistles which emanated from all of them seemed totally incongruous on all but the smallest engines.

France was a much less significant exporter of locomotives than Germany, but miniature versions of typical French classes went to Indo-China, French Equatorial Africa and Argentina as well as to other areas where France had interests. Fully fledged main-liners went to Algeria and Tunisia—which were under French rule—in addition to Turkey, where some lines were built with French capital. Among the last French exports were a class of huge 2–8–4s of typical domestic appearance for the Leopoldina Railway in Brazil.

Compounding became something of a religion within French locomotive practice and the principle was still adhered to when, after the advent of superheating, most of the world abandoned it. There were several reasons why this was so: first, trains were restricted to 75 miles an hour for many years by government rule; second, the loading gauge—though not as free as the American— was not as constricted as the British, and four-cylinder engines to the de Glehn system could be built without difficulty. Furthermore it is said that a French love of complexity committed them to compounding; drivers were given an engineer's training and were able to nurse the very best performance from their intricate steeds. Indeed, the Gallic temperament seemed unsuited to simplicity.

The de Glehn compound system was also tried in Britain, America, Prussia, Belgium, Switzerland, Portugal, Egypt and India—either by adoption or within exported French designs. Nowhere was it to have any long-term effect; if compounds used less fuel, simples required less maintenance and most countries opted for the latter in preference to fuel economy.

A more significant contribution to locomotive development was the Mallet, patented by Anatole Mallet in 1884 and first appearing as a 60 cm four-cylinder compound tank engine in which the driving wheels were split into two groups—the rear set in a rigid frame and the leading set in an articulated frame. The Mallet became widely adopted for working over lightly laid and sharply curved tracks, as it had a light axle loading in relation to power output and an ability to negotiate tight curves. Both tank and tender versions—simple and compound—appeared on many gauges, and over 5,000 locomotives are believed to have been built to the principle, 3,500 of them in the USA, where the type found its ultimate flowering.

Exciting developments occurred during the late 1920s when the French engineer Andre Chapelon greatly improved the steam locomotive's efficiency with a range of detailed internal modifications involving draughting, superheating and steam passages. Chapelon's work with steam traction was welcomed world wide.

However, World War II interrupted the French programme. At the end of the war over 1,300 chunky two-cylinder Mikados were supplied to the French railways by North American builders. These sprightly 2–8–2s, though lacking the smoothness of the French thorough-bred designs, needed far less maintenance and, in the face of impending electrification as the nation's railways were rebuilt, ironically brought the steam epoch to a close.

An amazing family of engines emerged from the Austro-Hungarian Empire, which prior to World War I covered a large area of eastern Europe. In 1891 the now legendary Karl Golsdorf was appointed Chief Mechanical Engineer of the Austrian State Railway and over the following 25 years he created 50 different designs, some of which remained in evidence in parts of Europe until the closing years of steam.

Not only were Golsdorf's designs revolutionary by European standards, but also many were built in vast numbers and some classes were constructed for up to 25 years after his death in 1916. Golsdorf's designs were largely conditioned by the light curving tracks and frail bridges which abounded in the Empire's territory and he was obliged to keep axle weights under 14 tons. This necessity—combined with a demand for adequate adhesion, for both heavy hauling and surmounting gradients—led to his use of many axles.

By the turn of the century his Classic 170 Class 2–8–0s and 180 Class 0–10–0s were in operation and by 1911 twelve-coupled power was reached. The long wheelbases were made laterally flexible and the leading pony was often tucked under the boiler to even out the weight distribution. This feature gave many Austrian classes a characteristic appearance of jutting forward. Golsdorf was a great believer in compounding, but following the advent of superheating the general trend was towards simples.

Austrian engines were liberally festooned with some quite bizarre features: double-domed boilers with an external connecting pipe; flared backplates to stovepipe chimneys—which had spark-averting meshes mushrooming from them; brake pumps, water purifiers and centrally opening smokebox doors; all combined to produce some of the most thrilling engines the world has ever seen. Their angular lines were laced beautifully by a brass band encircling the chimney.

When the Austrian Empire was split up after World War I, Czechoslovakia, Poland, Romania and Yugoslavia all inherited Austrian designs and building continued. Eventually, Poland, Romania and Yugoslavia gravitated towards German thinking, leaving Austria and Czechoslovakia to perpetuate the Golsdorf line.

The upheavals of two world wars spread Austrian locomotives throughout many European countries, while during the inter-war period batches of 0–10–0s and 2–10–0s were sent to Greece for freight and passenger work, respectively. After a distinguished working career, many of these survived to be among the last steam locomotives on the Hellenic State Railways.

In contrast, the Italian school remained within its domestic limits and exerted little influence beyond. The Italian State Railway was formed as early as 1905 and a range of twelve standard types was conceived by Giuseppe Zara, former Chief Mechanical Engineer of the Adriatic system. Zara's national standardization plan consisted largely of 2–6–0s, 2–6–2s and 2–8–0s of very moderate dimensions and was years ahead of similar schemes in Germany or Britain. Steam building in Italy ceased as early as the 1920s, owing to electrification, although many of the standard designs remained in widespread use until the 1970s.

The engines were characterized by spring balance safety valves, stovepipe chimneys, coned smokebox doors, round-topped fireboxes and cabs devoid of side windows. Although Italian locomotives themselves remained insular, the country's engineers contributed two developments—Caprotti valve gear and the Franco Crosti boiler. This latter innovation was heralded as being capable of attacking once and for all the steam locomotive's low thermal efficiency.

A fascinating sequel to the Italian story was the sudden building in 1953 of 20 enormous 2–10–2s by Breda of Milan for the Greek railways. These mammoths were designed almost 30 years after regular steam building in Italy ceased, and, with little tradition behind them, it is hardly surprising that the engines were not successful.

In the European nations not already mentioned little long-term distinction can be discerned. Holland, Belgium, Switzerland, Scandinavia and Spain fall within this category. Belgian builders exported a wide variety of locomotives, and in Holland some shapely exports were undertaken by Werkspoor of Amsterdam. Switzerland also featured in the production of many types of engines from their SLM works at Winterthur—usually the designs followed French or German practice.

Locomotive building commenced in Spain during the 1920s and big eight-coupled power to carry heavy loads over hilly regions predominated to become the definitive Spanish type. Spain's eight-coupled tradition was brought to a magnificent close with the ten Confederation 4–8–4s built in 1955–6 and decked in green livery—the only modern Spanish locomotives so adorned.

Scandinavian builders exported little and the last steam engines to survive there were the Finnish family, which represented a mixture of American and European practices.

104   This strange engine was found shunting at Maribor Studenci station in Slovenia during my photographic adventures with the Yugoslav railway historian Tadej Bratè. Built in 1907, and typically German in design, she is a standard-gauge 0–6–0 T which formerly worked on the Austrian Sudbahn Railway. Classified 151, she is the only engine of her type on the Yugoslav State Railway.

106

105 This delightful engine, seen at Lucknow in Northern India, is decked in a riot of highly saturated hues, in accordance with traditional Hindu art. She is a member of the 5 ft 6 in gauge XT Class 0–4–2 T, which consisted of 77 engines. The first 57 were built in Germany by Krupp at Essen between 1929 and 1936, while the last 20 came from India's Ajmer Works between 1945 and 1950. They were the lightest engines in the 'X' Series, having an axle load of only 13½ tons, and it has been said that the cost of operating them was lower than on any other Indian locomotives. As their appearance indicates, the XTs were essentially branch-line engines, typically found in some rural retreat at the head of two passenger coaches and a goods van. Such trains disappeared from many parts of the world when the motor-car became a popular form of transport, but India's economy is a railway economy: the private motor-car barely exists and country branches freely abound.

106 The great Victorian engineer Isambard Kingdom Brunel stated that '. . . if you are going on a very short journey, you need not take your dinner with you or corn for your horse . . .'—an adage which fits these two Fireless locomotives perfectly. The concept of a steam engine without a fire is incongruous to most people, but the Fireless is ideal for shunting in works or factories which have a ready supply of steam. Steam is injected at high pressure into a storage vessel on the engine, and fed to the cylinders via a reducing valve in order to achieve a constant power output until a recharge becomes necessary. The two examples shown here work for the Ludlow jute mill, situated on the banks of the Hooghly River near Calcutta. On the left is No. 3, an 0–4–0 with a conventional chimney, and on the right is No. 1, also an 0–4–0 but with the chimney placed behind the cab roof. Both engines came from Orenstein and Koppel. Apart from their efficiency, these engines were a prudent choice for such industries as the jute industry, where sparks from a conventional engine could wreak havoc.

107   One of the most interesting evolutionary variations on the conventional locomotive was the steam tram. These fascinating machines, which proliferated on roadside tramways during the 19th century, are virtually extinct today, and only a handful survive—primarily in Java. This example was found active on a sugar plantation in central Paraguay. Built by Borsig of Berlin in 1910, the veteran originally worked through the streets of Buenos Aires prior to being pensioned off to the sugar fields of neighbouring Paraguay. The engine's duty is to convey wagon-loads of raw sugar from the factory up to the connection with the standard-gauge 'Edwardian' main line, which runs from Asunción to the Argentinian border. This picture shows her actually running over the main line, as, backed by a flaming sunset, she trundles home to her depot in the factory yard.·

107

108 The Paraguayan Chaco is a vast and remote scrubland with one claim to fame—it is the home of the mighty quebracho tree, from which the world obtains tannin for processing leather. Railways were built to convey the logs up to factories on the River Paraguay, along which the tannin was carried for hundreds of miles to the Atlantic Ocean at Buenos Aires. Tannin was Paraguay's export gift to the world, but today it is manufactured synthetically and, one by one, these little railways in the middle of nowhere have closed down. Only one survives. No trains on the system need a whistle after dark, as the engines throw clouds of crimson embers 100 feet into the air and the trains can be seen approaching through the black Chaco night from a distance of 10 miles. The engine shown is named 'Laurita'; she is a 2 ft 6 in gauge 0–4–0 well tank believed to have been built by Arthur Koppel of Berlin in 1898. This typical German industrial carries an inscription on her side proclaiming in Spanish 'Primera Locomotora del Chaco Paraguayo'—the first locomotive on the Paraguayan chaco.

108

109

110   During the summer of 1977, the world's last high-speed steam trains gave way to diesels on the main line between Berlin and Dresden in East Germany. Until that time, the handsome 01 Pacifics of 1925—along with their rebuilt version the 01⁵s—were working passenger trains of up to 500 tons weight on timings faster than a mile a minute with top speeds of 90 miles an hour. These performances attracted enormous attention from enthusiasts, and the relaxed attitude adopted by the East German authorities towards railway photography meant that visitors from all over Europe were able to pay their last respects. Although the rebuilt 01⁵s have a sleek modernity, the original 01s, complete with huge windshields, were the favourites. By 1938, 241 had been built as the standard express passenger engine for Germany. They have a dashing elegance which is the hallmark of the Pacific and to see their 6 ft 6¾ in driving wheels spinning at speed is an unforgettable experience. Here one is depicted near Bhola with a Dresden-bound express. Displacement from the top duties was not the end; both variations continued to work elsewhere and in 1980 they were reported on passenger service between Saalfeld and Leipzig.

109   Germany's first 2–10–0 appeared in 1915 as the three-cylinder G12, a class which eventually numbered 1,500 engines. These superb locomotives could haul 1,000 ton trains over 1 in 200 gradients at 25 miles an hour and were the immediate forerunners of the even more numerous 44 Class three-cylinder 2–10–0s, introduced in 1926. The upheavals of two world wars spread the G12s to many countries. The picture shows one emerging from a tunnel on the Nova Gorica–Sežana line in Slovenia, northern Yugoslavia. Although the class disappeared from Slovenia during the mid-1970s, a few G12s still survive in East Germany under their old Reichbahn classification 58. However, these have been rebuilt with new boilers and tenders, while the conjugated valve gear of the original design has been replaced by an extra set of Walschaerts. East Germany also retains some active 44s.

110

'the last outpost of Prussian steam?'

111

111   A Prussian-type G8² 2–8–0 shunts at Armutçuk Colliery on the line radiating from Ereğli on Turkey's Black Sea coast. This short network is completely divorced from the remainder of Turkey's railway system and is worked by three G8²s, which were conveyed by ship from Zonguldak. A well-equipped workshop at Ereğli ensures that the locomotives do not have to be changed very frequently. The duty of these G8²s is to convey coal from Armutçuk Colliery over the 17 km line to Ereğli, whence the coal either goes to the huge steelworks or is exported from the docks. This line provides the perfect setting for observing these Prussian engines in action; the route follows the sea and 1 in 40 gradients occur along the coastal alignment. Much of the journey is through idyllic landscape; curves, tunnels and bridges abound, and these, combined with heavy grades, over which the engines work full throttle, render the line perfect for railway photography. In many ways this system is a miniature version of Brazil's Teresa Cristina Railway, discussed in Chapter 3—the isolation and *raison d'être* of the two networks being identical. As the Teresa Cristina has become the last stronghold of big American steam, possibly Ereğli will become the last outpost of Prussian steam.

112 East Germany has become celebrated for its narrow-gauge lines and few are more revered that the 23 km branch from Wolkenstein to Jöhstadt. Built to a gauge of 75 cm, the line is noted for its 0–4–4–0 Saxon Meyers supplied by Hartmann between 1892 and 1921. These engines date from the time of the Saxon State Railway, on which the Meyer type was widely used in order to negotiate tight curves. The engine shown is an 0–4–4–0 four-cylinder compound tank with its cylinders placed at the inner ends of two articulated power bogies—a system which enables the steam delivery pipe from the dome to be relatively short. The Meyer might be compared to the Fairlie, but it has the disadvantage of a restricted ashpan and firebox. This problem was solved by Kitson of Leeds, who designed Meyers with their bogies spread further apart and the firebox placed in between; this variation was called the Kitson Meyer (see Plate 38). Wolkenstein's Meyers are distinctive in carrying standard-gauge wagons on 75 cm gauge transporters, and it is a comical sight to watch these diminutive engines huffing and puffing along with an entourage of wagons almost twice their height.

113

114

113 These condensing 4–8–4s are one of the most significant locomotive types of the 20th century. They were built for service over the waterless Karroo desert of South Africa in 1953, following experiments carried out in 1949 by Henschel of Germany. The operation of these South African giants, which are classified 25, is fascinating. After the steam has driven the pistons, it activates a fan blower to provide the necessary draught in the smokebox before passing to condensing elements set in the tender. The condensate is fed back into the boiler and the engines can run for 700 miles without replenishment of water; their huge condensing tenders account for more than half the locomotive's 110 foot length. Their 70 square foot grate area is mechanically stoked. The locomotives weigh 234 tons in full working order. Built principally by North British of Glasgow, these condensers are the only pear-fronted engines in the world.

114 The front end of a Turkish Railways 2–8–2, one of eleven built by Henschel in 1937 for express passenger work. These engines are a typical German design of the inter-war period and were delivered along with a class of 2–10–0s, the two types having many interchangeable parts.

115 The German 'Kriegslokomotive' 2–10–0—or 'war engine', as it is known—is by far the most famous European steam locomotive type. It worked throughout Europe and beyond, and still survives today—as witness this splendid example belonging to the Turkish State Railways. She is one of a class consisting of about 50 engines. The 'Kriegslokomotive' originated in the two-cylinder 50 Class 2–10–0, which appeared as a standard Reichsbahn design in 1938. These engines were intended for lighter and more general work than the three-cylinder 44 Class 2–10–0s, but the demands of World War II necessitated an austerity version of the 50s, and from 1942 production switched to the 'Kriegslokomotive'. In all, over 10,000 engines were built to the basic 50 design and over 6,000 of them were 'Kriegslokomotives'. The German 2–10–0 epoch spans two world wars and involves a complex pattern of builders—often in occupied countries. The distribution of the various classes and their detail design features are as complex as that of any family of locomotives in history.

'the most famous
European steam locomotive type'

116 A scene at Santa Fé shed on Argentina's metre-gauge Belgrano Railway. The engine, No. 4606, is a 10A Class 2–6–2, built by Société Suisse in 1909 for the one-time French-owned Santa Fé Railway. The telephone has rung in the shed foreman's office; it is the yard superintendent: 'Our diesel has failed', he says. 'Have you a standby steam engine?' The foreman offers No. 4606 and the spare crew jump aboard the engine and turn on the oil jets, for steam must be raised in haste. After ten minutes, during which clouds of black oil smoke envelop the depot yard, 4606's safety valves lift at 175 pounds per square inch and the 70-year-old Swiss-built veteran is ready to take over the yard shunt—after she has towed the failed diesel back to the shed!

118 The ultimate in Spanish steam traction took the form of ten of these splendid oil-burning 5 ft 6 in gauge Class 242F 4–8–4 'Confederations', built by Maquinista in Barcelona in 1955–6. Their boilers were identical with those of the company's earlier 241F 4–8–2s of 1944. Superficially, these 'Confederations' remind one of the ex-LMS Duchess Class; certainly they were approximately the same size. Their original duty was to work heavy expresses between Ávila and Alsasua—the section of the Madrid–Irún main line which was not electrified. Electrification finally ousted them from this duty and they ended their days working freight trains from Miranda. These 'Confederations' were the last big steam locomotives to survive in western Europe, and they attracted enthusiasts from many different countries.

116

117 A handsome engine photographed in the early morning at the Cadem sheds in Damascus. Built by Hartmann of Germany in 1918 as a 2–8–2, she works the 3 ft 5⅜ in gauge Hedjaz Railway between Damascus and the Jordanian border at Der'ā. This section is part of the famous pilgrim line to Mecca authorized by the Sultan of Turkey to carry Moslems to their holy city. In the event, however, the line never progressed beyond the Arabian town of Medina. Originally, twelve of these Mikados worked the line but only five remain operable today, all in Syria.

119 Examples from one of Europe's most celebrated steam types are seen here awaiting repair at Linz depot, Austria, in 1972. They are members of the former 629 Class of superheated 4–6–2 Ts introduced by the Austrian Sudbahn Railway in 1913 for suburban and cross-country work. They proved to be excellent performers and their 13 ton axle loading ensured widespread distribution. After the Austrian Empire was split up following World War I, some 629s were inherited by Czechoslovakia, and the Skoda works continued to build them up until 1941. In the much shrunken Austria building continued under the Federal Railways until 1927. The type also occurred in Hungary and Poland. During the Nazi occupation of Austria the 629s received the classification 77, which they retained after the occupation had ended. After the war five passed to Yugoslavia as part of a reparation package. Classified 18, these engines remained at work until 1973 hauling passenger trains from Maribor to Blieburg.

119

120 Steam development in Finland came to an end with two standard designs which were entirely Finnish in concept: the HR1 Pacific and the TR1 Mikado. As might be expected, the two classes looked remarkably similar and had many common parts, including boiler, windshields, cab and eight-wheeled bogie tenders. The majority were built in Finland, at either Tampella or Lokomo Oy, although 20 TR1s were obtained from the German works of Jung in 1953. Building of the two classes spanned the 20 year period between 1937 and 1957. Dieselization caused the Pacifics to be withdrawn prematurely, but many TR1s survived into the 1970s, and the picture shows one boiling up at Kouvola amid a wintry landscape. They are a typical mixed-traffic design of the years leading up to World War II and were easily capable of working 1,500 ton trains over level routes. I regard these engines with special affection as I travelled the footplate on one of their last duties. The train was an engineer's special from Rovaniemi bound for Raajarvi quarries, 40 miles beyond the Arctic Circle in Lapland.

120

121 The Prussian school of locomotive design is one of the most significant in the history of our subject. From the turn of the century, many standard Prussian classes were built in large numbers and, upon the unification of Germany following World War I, they provided a backbone for the famous Reichsbahn standards built from the 1920s onwards. One of the milestones in Prussian locomotive design was the three-cylinder G12 Class 2–10–0, the forerunner of the 44 class. The G12s first appeared in 1915, and in 1919 a powerful two-cylinder 2–8–0 appeared, classified G8², which was a shortened version of them; this is the type of engine illustrated here. The G12, G8² and 44 Classes all look very similar. Between them they once totalled little short of 5,000 engines. The engine shown is one of a batch of 62 G8²s built for Turkey between 1927 and 1935 by Nohab and Tubize.

122 Indonesia provides a superb hunting ground for German industrial steam; the sugar plantations of Java and the palm oil estates of Sumatra are host to hundreds of locomotives. These plantation engines are particularly efficient ecologically; the palm oil engines of Sumatra burn nutshells, while the sugar plantation engines of Java burn bagasse. The picture reveals a typical plantation scene as a 700 mm gauge bagasse-burning 0–8–0 tender tank heads towards the Pesantren sugar factory with a rake of freshly cut cane. This engine, named 'Dieng' after the famous plateau in central Java, was built by Orenstein and Koppel in 1922.

123 This 600 mm gauge 0–4–0 well tank, built in Germany by Orenstein and Koppel during the early years of the century, works at a stone quarry in Uruguay. Many German industrials are of the well tank type in which water is carried between the engine's frame. This method contrasts with the common British and American practice of carrying water on saddle tanks slung either side of the engine's boiler. Originally a coal burner, the engine has now been converted to oil firing and the fuel is carried in the huge drum placed above the boiler—one tankful enabling the engine to work for eight hours. The purpose of the amazing railway (less than half a mile in length) on which this engine works is to convey stone up to the connection with the standard-gauge main line. The stone is used as track ballast, and, according to the quarry engineer, the engine has been engaged upon this work for over half a century.

122

123

124 The sleek greyhound lines of this striking engine are still in evidence despite its moribund condition. She is one of 20 four-cylinder compound Pacifics built for the Dutch East Indies by Werkspoor of Amsterdam between 1917 and 1922. For many years these engines worked the expresses over the 3 ft 6 in gauge east–west main line between Batavia (Jakarta) and Surabaya in Java. They were classified C53 under the Indonesian State Railways. After their displacement by diesels the C53s were relegated to working local trains. Throughout the 1970s, examples could be found languishing in mature graveyards like this one at Madiun.

124

125 The heat in the Syrian capital, Damascus, during high summer is almost intolerable. On Friday, the Moslem day of rest, many inhabitants take excursion trains up into the cool hills which surround the city. The route traversed is part of the former Damascus–Beirut line, which crosses the towering Lebanon Range. In recent years the trains from Damascus have terminated at Sergayah, a green oasis on the Lebanese border where a few hours of relief can be gained from the searing heat. The railway was constructed to the unique Levantine gauge of 3 ft 5⅜ in by a French company under Ottoman concessions in 1895 and the same locomotives which were built for the line in 1894 remain in full command today. They consist of Swiss-built 2–6–0 Ts and 0–6–2 Ts which work from Cadem shed in Damascus; they are all oil-fired and make a spectacular sight smokily toiling their way through the golden hills.

125

126 Few people would expect to find a steam tram active in West Germany but this delightful engine can be found at Lake Chiemsee, near Salzburg on the German–Austrian border. The engine works on the Chiemseebahn, which runs from Stock, on the lakeside, up to Prien, where the line joins the German Federal Railway. Today this standard-gauge branch is used by tourists visiting the lake. The locomotive is an 0–4–0 type built specially for the line by Krauss of Munich in 1887.

127

127   The engine crossing this bridge, at Hyrynsalmi in the northeast of Finland, is the last working survivor of the Finnish Railway's Jumbo Class—a set of 142 heavy goods engines introduced by Finland's Tampella works in 1917. This relatively straightforward picture took five hours to make. Almost three hours were spent in reaching the camera position from the track, as the snow had drifted against the railway embankments to depths of 12 feet. I then stood for a further two hours, shoulder deep in snow, waiting for the Jumbo to roll across the bridge.

128   One of 20 giant 2–10–2s supplied to the Greek Railways in 1953–4 by the Italian builders Breda and Ansaldo. There was certainly a need for such engines on the Greek main line from Athens to Salonika, but why the order was placed in Italy has mystified railway historians ever since. The country had never built such large engines before, nor had they built any main-line steam locomotives for more than 25 years. Troubles were inevitable. At one time the 2–10–2s were taken out of traffic for modifications but, sadly, the problems were too fundamental to rectify. For the enthusiast, however, these amazing Santa Fés added further fascination to Greece's already cosmopolitan stable of engines. After dieselization of the top duties, the 2–10–2s were demoted, and although they could be extremely fleet-footed with moderate trains, an early withdrawal was inevitable. On my last visit to Greece in 1979, I saw a batch of them being cut up north of Athens—next to the very main line which once held such high hopes for their prowess.

'the country had never built
such large engines before'

129 No. 91, the last survivor of a class of 2–8–0s built by Hartmann of Chemnitz early this century for the Hedjaz Railway, known as the pilgrim route to Mecca. She is seen at Cadem shed in Damascus—the depot which provides the motive power for Syria's sections of the Hedjaz. The route is built to the Levantine gauge of 3 ft 5⅜ in.

130 As the last West European country to dispense with steam traction, Portugal became a Mecca for enthusiasts, offering vintage steam on two gauges. Latter-day steam operations centred around the 5 ft 6 in gauge Douro Valley line, which ran eastwards from Oporto to Barca d'Alva on the Spanish frontier. This route was joined at four separate points by metre-gauge feeders. These 2–8–0s first appeared as a class of eleven engines for Portugal's State-owned Sul e Sueste Railway from Schwartzkopf of Berlin in 1912–13, and a further seven engines followed from North British in 1921. Their 13¾ ton axle load gave them an excellent route availability and they were found on various parts of the system until the end of steam. The example shown is No. 710—a Schwartzkopf engine of 1913. She is seen in the heart of the Douro Valley at Regua—a once-famous gathering point for enthusiasts from all over the world.

129

130

131 In her day this lovely French 2–8–0 would have been ordinary enough, but now she represents an almost extinct phase of European locomotive design. Built for Turkey's Smyrna Cassaba et Prolonguements Railway, the engine, along with eleven sisters, came from Humboldt of Paris in 1912. The veteran is seen at Izmir (formerly known as Smyrna) waiting to take an evening suburban train to Buca. Izmir, situated on Turkey's Ægean coast, was a fine place to observe suburban steam trains during the late 1970s, and two of these Humboldts worked turn about with ex-Prussian G8s and G10s. As the trains left the city, they climbed past a remarkable backdrop of suburbs with houses perched on every conceivable inch of the hillsides.

THE
FATE OF STEAM

The steam locomotive was surely man's most animated creation and its diverse personality was, from the outset, guaranteed to capture the popular imagination. However, having provided man with his most civilized form of land transportation, the time came when the steam engine had to go. Sadness was felt on all sides, from official circles right down to the men in the breakers' yards, but the tide of what was called economic efficiency could not be stemmed. After an agonizing decline spanning two decades, most western nations witnessed the one truly living machine slip into history. In Britain letters to the national press and magazines complained that life would be intolerable without the steam engine. A few people even emigrated.

There has been much debate about the wisdom of dispensing with steam. Obviously the road and oil lobbies have vested interests in running down both the railway and the steam locomotive—one recalls the harebrained movement of the 1950s to convert Britain's railways into roads. Unfortunately, in many countries the antirailway lobbies have been frighteningly successful.

In Britain the railway hierarchy decided that in view of the tremendous competition from road and air—combined with the deprivations resulting from World War II—a whole new image (that glib word of the 1950s) was required. There was no place for a smoke-spewing kettle on wheels. The metaphor was totally inappropriate, but the image-makers, having destroyed thousands of fine locomotives, some only a few years old, declared that none should be allowed to foul the nation's tracks again.

A different situation existed in America, where it was claimed that steam had reached the loading gauge limits and was not capable of further development. It was also claimed that the nature of the work was no longer acceptable; that driving, firing and servicing were dirty and antisocial; that problems with labour recruitment were looming. Even in Brazil, a medical report dated 1978 indicted the Teresa Cristina Railway's steam policy and the adverse conditions to which crews were exposed. It cited seven principal hazards: 'trepidation, vibration, sound pollution, thermic overload, vicious positions, coal dust and excessive light from the firebox'. These claims were verified after the crew's health had been monitored by audiometry, X-rays and ophthalmological and clinical examinations. The conclusions were: '. . .highly insalubrious service and that elimination of the problem within the steam locomotive's design inexist'. Many an old engine driver enjoying his retirement after a lifetime of 'vicious positions' could only give a wry smile at such a prognosis. And whatever the vicissitudes, a steam engine represented a challenge that brought the best out in the crew and helped engender pride in the job—an element almost entirely lacking today.

I will never lose my memories of Britain during the 1950s, when the nation had a fully comprehensive railway network operated by steam engines burning home coal. Services were frequent and relatively fast; few people experienced any difficulty in travelling and safety was almost absolute. However, when the nation developed a mania for the popular motor car and road haulage became officially encouraged, the 'image-makers' destroyed a large percentage of the railway system—so crippling what remained—and, furthermore, adopted a form of motive power dependent upon foreign oil.

However, error is seldom universal; so why have railway administrations all over the world declared against steam? The short answer is that they haven't. Once the industrial nations had graduated to the manufacture of diesels, they persuaded the emergent lands, through either salesmanship, credit, loans or political manoeuvres, to accept the new traction, become up to date and move into the 20th century. Emotive talk; and few countries anxious to improve their lot resisted such offers.

Often the results were disastrous, complex diesels being delivered to areas devoid of oil and with a workforce far better suited to the operating of steam, with all its simplicity, longevity and ability to burn locally available fuels. Yet from the mid-1950s the entire world went diesel-mad with all the trendiness of a universal pop mania; every nation, regardless of indigenous conditions, had to get rid of steam as quickly as possible.

The advocates of steam state that many further improvements are possible within the basic Stephensonian concept; and, given today's technological advance, this is obviously true. The Garratt principle, for example, offers untapped possibilities as far as loading gauge limits are concerned.

As a regular visitor to India to see work currently being done by steam, one does escape the brainwashing and realize—if one ever really forgot—that its performance and reliability are anything but outdated.

132

132 The poignant end of British inside-cylinder 0—6—0s at a breaker's yard in Northern India. Gone now the clanging shovel and gone the sweet sooty emanations of oil and steam; gone the living spirit of man's most animated machine. Gone to a jigsaw in iron and steel are those whose wheels have come full circle.

Further credence is lent to such claims, of course, by the problem of world oil. One would have thought that the horror-filled scaremongering which has been rife over the past five years would be sufficient to precipitate a world-wide shift from road to rail and from diesel to steam. Incredibly, no such proposals have been mooted—that is, until recently. Even politically vulnerable South Africa, with its plenitude of cheap coal and labour, and not a drop of oil in sight, has pursued a relentless policy of dieselization. However, the tide may be starting to turn. China, Zambia and Zimbabwe, to mention three countries, are involved in a partial reversion to steam and there are signs that India is beginning to retract some of her conversion programme.

But the renaissance has barely begun and over the past 20 years the world's railways have been studded with derelict locomotives either languishing in broken-down depots or standing in forlorn lines. Most reach the breaker's yard within a year of withdrawal, but others lie abandoned, seemingly forgotten by the world at large.

In certain countries—particularly the communist states—many withdrawn engines have been 'mothballed' for possible future use in an emergency. These strategic reserves are based upon sound reasoning, and it is surprising that few of the western democracies have adopted a similar system. However, rumour has been rife about large numbers of engines hidden on mountainsides or in old tunnels, especially in Britain, where people have even claimed knowledge of such reserves. Unfortunately, the facts do not bear out the stories.

As in the natural order, where survival goes to the most adaptable species, the highly specialized locomotives— the heavy main-line passenger and freight classes—were the first to go, being too large, too heavy or simply too uneconomical to be utilized on lesser work. By contrast, the older main-line types, though long since outclassed in the power stakes, are invariably suitable for alternative duties; the passenger engines move to branch lines and the freight designs gravitate to pick-up goods or shunting. Such engines often take on a new lease of life in industrial service; instances of this can be found all over the world and several have been mentioned in this book.

The mixed-traffic engine in the form of Moguls and various eight-coupleds has also caused the more specialized types to disappear, and many administrations have whittled down their steam fleets to a few standard types—such engines as 2–8–2s and 4–8–2s—with a mean driving wheel diameter of 5 ft 3 in.

But many veterans survive and their longevity is held in respectful awe. To see an engine almost a century old still puffing around and doing useful work is an inspiring sight to behold. Like the proverbial Irishman's gun, many have been rebuilt or have received new parts to a point of their original identity disappearing; but others survive virtually as built, even their boiler shells being original.

133   Having spent half a century hauling 1,500 ton coal trains over the hill regions of Bengal, an Indian Railways XE Class 2–8–2 reaches its sad end. Labourers manually hack off the boiler rivet heads—20 vicious back-breaking blows being needed to remove each one. The foreground is dominated by aspects of the subject's anatomy, which can be enumerated one by one: a crank axle, a dome cover, a piston, a chimney, cylinder valves, driving wheel fragments, springs and a buffer.

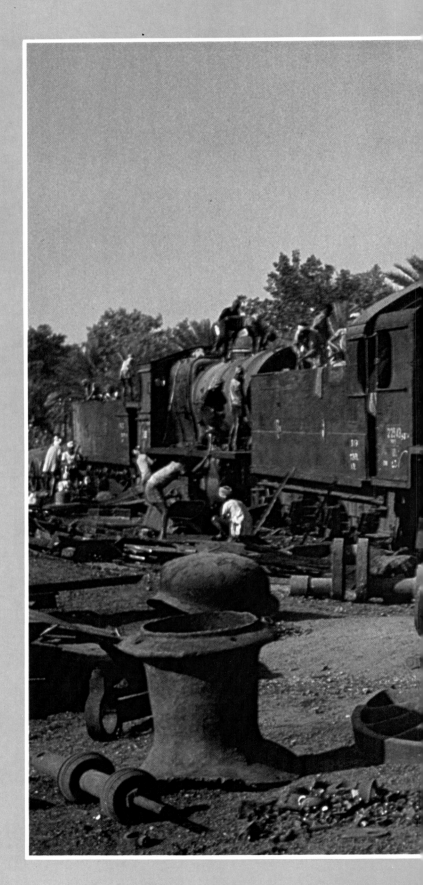

'vicious back-breaking blows'

134

134 The signing ceremony has been completed and this Indian Railways XE Class 2–8–2, built on the Clyde in 1930 by Beardmore for the East Indian Railway, now belongs to the scrap contractors. The gruesome task of breaking up begins in earnest, and within two days this proud locomotive will be reduced to a heap of scrap metal.

135 Under the burning mid-day sun of northern India, a workman uses an acetylene torch to cut up the wheels of a British-built 0–6–0, while the next engine to be scrapped looms impressionistically in the background. Even in India, with its plenitude of coal and labour, the steam locomotive—with all its inbuilt simplicity and longevity—is destined to pass to an early grave.

136–141 (overleaf) The heart-rending decline of steam was characterized by dumps of moribund engines, and the steam locomotive, which once imparted such joyous animation to the railway network, was reduced to a lifeless ghost. In many cases the rusted hulks lingered on for years—as if the curtain was reluctant to fall on so great a dynasty. The steam locomotive's death brought to a close one of the most dramatic periods in the history of transport. Furthermore, it marked the end of an entire social order wherein the previously manageable pace of daily life was shattered by the turmoils engendered in an economy based on road transport. It was ironic that the death of steam, justified on the grounds of increased efficiency, should in fact coincide with a drastic reduction in much of the world's railway network. Sometimes the dumped engines, instead of simply contrasting with the new motive power, actually became memorials to the decline of whole railway systems.

Engines in scrapyards evoke many images and emotions. One thinks of the men who toiled—often with immense pride—to build the locomotives, lavishing on them a standard of workmanship which enabled many to remain at work for nearly a century. The huge foundries, from which engines rolled in their thousands, have, in most cases, also disappeared, though their names are now a revered part of industrial history. Steam's graveyards have all the trappings of exquisite sadness: the shattered windows of closed depots, tangled vegetation around rusting ironmongery, and pieces of old locomotives lying on the ground like the bones of a dinosaur. No-one who loved locomotives can remain unmoved by such scenes—scenes which many of us thought would never occur in our lifetime. But it is decreed that all forms of creation possess inherent defects which, in a changing environment, make their ultimate disappearance inevitable—sadly, the steam locomotive was no exception to this rule.

142 It is 1968 and the steam age in Great Britain has ended. Those engines that remain lie cold and derelict, waiting to be towed away to breakers' yards. Many of the great steam sheds—once vibrant and bustling elements of the nation's transportation system—became mausoleums to a bygone industrial age. Such was the case at Patricroft in Manchester, where a Stanier 8F 2–8–0 of the 1930s here stands condemned alongside a British Railways Standard 5 Caprotti 4–6–0

142

143 Acetylene sparks fly as the worker, bent upon his task like a medieval executioner, cuts up the driving axle of a Stanier Black 5 4–6–0. These engines were among the last to work in Britain, and this study, made at Cohen's scrapyard in Kettering, symbolizes the death of the steam age in the land of its birth.

144 The derelict structures of man's industrial past dominate the foreground as a Hunslet-type Austerity 0–6–0 saddle tank clanks a string of wagons back to the pithead at Hafod-rhy-nys in South Wales. The world's first steam locomotive was born in an adjacent valley in 1804. The colour camera now records the end of the epoch. The semi-derelict, slag-ridden valleys bear witness to a revolution spent; the waters wash timelessly down the valley sides and the skies of South Wales seem perennially grey.

143

145

145 A picture that might be called 'The Last Sunset', in which the sun's dying glow is mocked by the flare of the acetylene torch as the sole surviving Indian Railways GC1 Class 2–8–0 is cut up at Jamalpur. First introduced in 1906 for the East Indian Railway, these typically Edwardian locomotives resemble the later Great Central 2–8–0s which once whistled their way over the Pennines between Sheffield and Manchester.

146 This shapely 4–4–0 was discovered on a children's playground in Brazil. The engine was painted in gaudy colours in an endeavour to amuse the local children; but once the novelty had worn off, the veteran became derelict. She is one of a class built during the late 19th century by Sharp Stewart of Glasgow for hauling passenger trains over Brazil's Mogiana Railway. A sister engine in its full working glory is shown in Plate 32.

146

147 The breaker's yard is the sad but inevitable end for 99 per cent of the world's surviving steam locomotives. Happily, this historic engine is one of the exceptions. She is safely tucked away in the roundhouse at Leicester, where local volunteers have started restoration. She is an 0–8–0 formerly owned by the London and North Western Railway, or 'Premier Line', as it was popularly called. The saving of this engine was fortuitous, as few locomotives from this famous railway have been preserved, and their absence creates a serious gap in the ranks of surviving British steam.

147

Today, however, the threat of the graveyard looms over every engine, whatever its status, and all over the world these moribund dumps of engines testify to the end of a dynasty—industrial monuments as poignant and stark in form as the Acropolis of Athens. The silent tomblike atmosphere of the locomotive graveyard is intense— the very converse of spirited animation. When one is in these places, one feels that the engines are actually aware of human presence. Locomotive graveyards are adventure playgrounds for young and old alike; to clamber into a cab and gaze ahead through the smashed and jagged fragments of the spectacle glasses is to imagine the engine back in its full working glory.

One yearns to provide that vital charge of fire and water which would allow the rusted hulks to clank their way out of the graveyard. Few condemned engines are beyond repair, and thousands run to the dump under their own steam. In many parts of the world railway preservationists are resurrecting locomotives. In replacing death with life, they cheat the passing of time and achieve, for the engine, one of man's deepest yearnings—immortality. Only the other day an article in my local paper read: 'Old faithful steams to the rescue', recounting how the resurrected Jubilee Class 'Leander', while out on a rail tour, was summoned to help a stricken diesel in the wilds of Cumberland.

The first preservation scheme in Britain was born in 1950, when a fund was set up to save the Talyllyn Railway in Wales; many greeted the idea with cynical scepticism—enthusiasts could never run a railway, they claimed. Spurred by the success of the Talyllyn project, more schemes were set up, and as the nationalized system abandoned branch lines dedicated bands of enthusiasts took them over. When steam finished on British Railways in 1968, there remained a dump of over 200 engines at Woodham's scrapyard in Barry. This natural reserve provided a breathing space for funds to be raised, and during the 1970s over 100 engines were rescued, including many famous types.

Fortunately, steam's passing coincided with a period in which the means were available for preservation. In Britain and elsewhere the ruling premise was that the engines selected for preservation by the state were unrepresentative of so great a heritage. Engines must survive in their full working glory, as opposed to being stuffed and mounted in a museum. It is fitting that Britain should lead the world in this field, and already over 1,600 locomotives have been saved. Some can now be seen heading rail tours over the state system. In America, these include photographic stops at suitable locations where the train runs past for the edification of travellers wielding batteries of cameras and tape recorders.

Preservation in the developing world is of a very different order. Railway enthusiasm as we know it does not exist, railways being not part of the indigenous culture but something grafted from outside. The circumstances in many rural economies, where the general level of education is poor, forbid interest in anything beyond the essentials of living. Even so, most governments retain some exhibits for their state museums, enhanced by the piecemeal efforts of various industries who delight in putting locomotives on plinths or among flower-beds in front of their head offices. Another favourite is the use of children's playgrounds as a last resting place. Apart from being an attractive toy, a locomotive is not too easy to vandalize once the novelty wears off. Thus, as an investment it makes a sensible addition to a leisure area.

In absolute contrast to these pleasant musings is the fate of the great majority—the cacophony of the breaker's yard. It is unfashionable for these places to be either photographed or written about, yet they form an intrinsic part of the drama. Even when being dismembered amid the wrench of tearing metal and stench of acetylene gas, the steam locomotive retains its majesty and dignity, like a proud nobleman being executed by an unruly mob. Amid a jigsaw in iron and steel a locomotive is reduced to sad piles of scrap—varying grades of metal to be resold at varying market prices.

What of the future? Will our subject, with its seemingly mystical ability to survive, ever stage a real comeback? In today's world few would refute the possibility. Yet, sadly, it seems unlikely to return in the same beloved form. A 1980 issue of the *Sunday Times* contained details of an articulated steam locomotive design prepared at an English university with the aid of computer techniques. Futuristic in its appearance, it is claimed to represent a plausible challenge to the diesel, and Australia, China and Argentina have expressed interest. With such brave concepts on the drawing-board, the world awaits developments with bated breath.

148 A scene which dramatically conveys the sad poetry of a locomotive graveyard. The location is northern India. Huge engines, abandoned years ago, slowly rot their way back into the earth. The ever-encroaching vegetation may cause the engines to be forgotten, only to be rediscovered by future generations as testimony to one of the most civilized forms of land transport man has yet devised.

'one of the most civilized
forms of land transport'

GLOSSARY

Articulation jointing of the normally rigid frame (see below) with one or more pivots, making it more flexible and enabling a locomotive to pass over sharper curves.

Axle-loading the weight imposed on the track by the heaviest pair of wheels; this influences the locomotive's route availability (see below).

Bar frame a frame (see below) built up from girders rather than steel plates.

Big three the three dominant American locomotive builders, Baldwin, Alco, and Lima.

Caprotti valve gear a mechanism for sequencing the admission and exhaustion of steam in a cylinder (see below), using cams as in a motor-car engine.

Class this is usually a specific design of locomotive within a broad type (see below).

Compound a locomotive in which steam is used twice, passing from a high-pressure cylinder to a larger low-pressure cylinder.

Condensing locomotive a rare type of locomotive, used in arid regions, which condenses its steam for re-use in the boiler as feedwater.

Conjugated valve gear a valve gear arrangement in which a central cylinder is served by levers connected to the valve gears of the outside cylinders.

Coupled axles the axles carrying the coupled wheels (see below).

Coupled wheels the driving wheels together with the wheels joined to them by the coupling rod. This arrangement enables the power to be spread over several wheels, thereby reducing wheel-slip.

Cowcatcher called a 'pilot' in America, this is a semi-vertical plate or grid above the rails at the front of the engine, designed to prevent obstructions like cattle being overrun and causing a derailment.

Cross-stretcher a transverse girder or plate joining the frame plates to ensure rigidity.

Cylinder the chamber into which high pressure steam is admitted to push the piston alternately backwards and forwards. The piston is connected by rods to the driving wheel and thereby turns it. Most locomotives have two cylinders but some have three or four.

Diagram a locomotive's work schedule.

Double-header a train with two locomotives at the head end.

Firebox the part of the boiler accommodating the grate and its surrounding water spaces.

Fireless a locomotive whose boiler is charged with steam from an outside source.

Footplate 1) the floor on which the locomotive crew stands 2) the running plate (see below).

Frame the box-form structure on which the boiler and wheels are mounted.

Franco-Crosti boiler a boiler in which exhaust steam passes through drums to pre-heat the feedwater.

Gauge the distance between the insides of the rails on straight track.

Grate area the size of the firebox interior at grate level in square feet or square metres, a common measure of steam-raising capability.

Inside-cylinder having two cylinders, both installed inside the frame.

Livery a railway's colour scheme for locomotives and rolling stock.

Outside-cylinder having all cylinders outside the frame.

Outside frame having the coupled wheels within the frame.

Outside valve gear the mechanism actuating the steam admission valves, and located outside the frame.

Plate frame frame (see above) based on two thick longitudinal steel plates resting on the main axles.

Route availability the freedom of a given locomotive class to run over tracks and structures of varying specifications, this being determined by its weight and other dimensions.

Running plate the footwalk along the sides and front of a locomotive's boiler.

Saddleback see **Saddletank**

Saddletank a locomotive carrying its water over its boiler in a saddle-shaped tank.

Sandbox a fixed container for sand, having a pipe enabling sand to be deposited in front of the coupled wheels when wheel-slip is likely.

Simple having simple expansion (single use) of the steam, as opposed to compound (see above).

Slide valve valve controlling steam admission to the cylinder and flat in form, in contrast to the more modern piston valve.

Smokebox the drum-shaped forward extension of the boiler accommodating the exhaust arrangement and steampipes. It has a frontal door through which the cinders are removed.

ST abbreviation for saddletank.

Superheating subjecting the steam on its way to the cylinders to a final high-temperature heating, in order to reduce subsequent condensation in the cylinders.

T abbreviation for tank locomotive.

Tank locomotive a locomotive designed without a tender (see below) and carrying its fuel and water in its own tanks and bunker.

Ten-coupled a locomotive with ten coupled wheels (see above).

Tender the vehicle attached to a locomotive to accommodate fuel and water.

Tracking a motoring term roughly equivalent to the railway term 'riding', a description of the ease with which a locomotive negotiates curved or imperfect track.

Tractive effort the force exerted by a locomotive on the couplings of the vehicle next to it; that is, a measure of pulling power.

Type usually a broad categorization relating to a locomotive's basic layout, especially its wheel arrangement (for explanation of wheel notation see below), and its function.

Vertical cylinder an unusual arrangement in which the cylinders are mounted high in a vertical position. Some of the very earliest locomotives were like this.

Walschaert's valve gear a mechanism actuating a locomotive's steam admission and exhaustion valves which was designed by the Belgian Walschaerts and became very widespread.

Wheel arrangement locomotive wheel arrangements are described by a three-figure notation, with the first figure indicating the number of leading (guiding) wheels, the second the number of large (coupled) wheels, and the third the number of trailing (supporting) wheels. Tender wheels are not counted and Garratt locomotives are treated as two locomotives linked by a plus sign. In America, and to a lesser extent elsewhere, different wheel arrangements have their own name; for example: Consolidation (2-8-0); Mikado (2-8-2); Santa Fé (2-10-2); Texas (2-10-4); Mogul (2-6-0); Atlantic (4-4-2); Pacific (4-6-2); Mountain)4-8-2); Confederation or Northern (4-8-4).

Well tank a tank locomotive (see above) carrying its water in a low-slung tank between the frames.

INDEX